Right Isn't Left

By
Brett Peterson

Dedicated to Cheston Moon.

Acknowledgment

This book is based on true life stories, and I couldn't have written it without life itself. I would like to thank the people in my life, especially my family, for enduring the events that involved you and your lives.

Special thanks to my father for building my character, good or bad.

CONTENTS

About the Author

Brett Peterson was born and raised in Idaho on a small farm with his family. He has owned several businesses in his life and taught school for over 20 years. He is retired and enjoying time with his family his dog, and trying to give readers life events from the colorful events in his 70 years of life. His vivid views and stories hope to educate the reader

Ranch Upbringing

Barry was born and raised in Southern Wyoming on a cattle ranch of over 500 acres. He was raised with his three sisters, a younger brother by eighteen years, a mother, and a father to whom Barry was extremely close.

At a very young age, he spent an enormous amount of time hanging out with his father. His father, Jacob, was a great person and a great father, but was stern and didn't allow any back talk. He was 6 feet tall, quite muscular, and had a demanding voice. When he was pissed—prepare. He expected 110% effort in everything you did and, along with that, near perfection in a finished project.

This story is about Barry and his lifelong battle with just doing what's right.

At a young age, Barry was on his own when it came to playing with other boys. Being born surrounded by all girls—both sisters and cousins—he hung out with his father and grandfather a lot. Sure, having a family full of girls teasing him was fantastic, but a need for male interaction was always a driving force. When the girls hung out with their grandmother, Barry usually went with his grandfather to work, and that could be anywhere from farming and mechanic work to the local bar.

Barry's grandfather was a gruff old guy, a former shipyard welder with a good desire for alcohol like a sailor; he cussed a lot and argued with anyone who would start a discussion.

Barry's father spent a lot of time with horses and tack, and Barry was next to him on most occasions. When Barry was five years old, his father, Jacob, got his leg caught in the PTO shaft of the grain auger. Jacob yelled at Barry to go grab his mother from the house to help shut off the tractor. Barry ran as fast as he could, although it seemed like forever to get to the house. He retrieved his mother and returned to the tractor. By the grace of God, the PTO shaft jarred loose, causing it to fall off the tractor, saving Jacob from losing his leg—although his lower leg was severely cut.

After a bunch of stitches and a few months of healing, Jacob's leg was back to normal. Jacob was so impressed by Barry's ability to run for help rather than freeze up that he purchased him a new bike.

Later that year, Jacob was training a horse to stay in a chute while throwing a lariat over its head. Jacob asked Barry to stand in the chute so the horse would know it shouldn't move forward, and he agreed. After a short time, the horse decided it had had enough and darted out of the loading chute, running over Barry in doing so. The horse trampled Barry as it escaped, breaking 5 ribs with cuts and bruises all over his body. As the horse exited the loading chute, it landed on Barry's bicycle, smashing it flat; it was destroyed. Jacob never replaced the bike, perhaps figuring it was a bad location for Barry to park his bike.

A few years later, Barry and his family attended a rodeo, where Jacob had competed. As they were leaving the event, they were pulled over by the police. Jacob's brake lights weren't functioning on the trailer, and the officer issued a ticket, saying it wasn't safe to drive home. Jacob explained to the officers that he couldn't just leave the horses on the side of the road because somebody couldn't see a bright white trailer behind his pickup. Things got heated, and Jacob was arrested for failure to conform, leaving Barry's mother and the children crying in the cab of the truck.

Barry was too young to understand why, but his mother was allowed to drive the truck back to the fairgrounds, where they left the trailer and horses for the night. Early the next morning, after Jacob returned home, Barry and his father went to retrieve the trailer and horses. Luckily, everything was fine. The trailer lights were still not working, but at least it was daylight.

A few years later, Barry and his father attended another rodeo that went late into the night. On the way home, a horse fell through the bottom of the trailer while they were traveling down the road. The trailer had a weak spot on the floor, allowing the horse's legs to fall through and make contact with the pavement.

Jacob immediately pulled over and screamed at Barry to stay in the pickup while he rushed to check on the animals. Moments later, he returned to grab a gun from behind the seat to put the horse down. It was a bad night for rodeo, a bad night for Barry and Jacob, and the grief lingered for months over the loss of a wonderful horse. Barry was learning at a young age that just because something is morally correct, it isn't always easy.

During the spring months, everything was in bloom, and summer was just around the corner. Like most animals, Jacob's horses enjoyed basking in the warm sun. After being fed in the morning, they grazed as usual, sampling various edible items for taste.

One tree stood in full bloom, its blossoms carrying a sweet but deadly taste. The horses, unaware of the danger, enjoyed snacking on the fruit of the locust tree. After a couple of hours of grazing on the blossoms, the horses in that pasture began dropping to the ground.

Jacob panicked. He could tell the animals were overheating, likely suffering from some kind of fever. Knowing he had no time to waste, he grabbed the tractor, secured straps around the horses, and dragged them across the pasture to the canal running along the north side. He hoped the cold water would lower their body temperatures in time.

Of the three horses that had consumed the blossoms, two survived the poisoning. One did not. The two horses that lived lost most of their hair due to the extreme fever. It was a hard lesson for everyone involved, but especially for Barry. From that moment on, he developed a deep desire to educate himself about poisonous plants.

Viking Rituals

Barry is always striving to educate himself, hoping to make his father proud and stand out in the family. Jacob, having spent his entire life on farms and ranches, firmly believes that rural kids are the smartest and toughest on the block.

Being left-handed presents an extra challenge for Barry, as it's not widely accepted in the real world at the time. He must learn to write, shoot a gun, play sports—and most importantly, do it well—because Jacob does not tolerate the phrase, *I can't do this.*

Barry learns to shoot very well, having to place a perfect shot, as he doesn't have the ability to load another shell without lowering the rifle. Barry must write with his left hand, which makes his schooling harder to achieve high grades.

Jacob was very good at baseball in his younger years of school; he had gone to college on a baseball scholarship. He had the highest RBI in the state for high school sports, and knew baseball very well, inside and out. Jacob was very determined to teach Barry the game of baseball, lefty or not.

Jacob made Barry play and act right-handed, telling Barry that a left-handed batter can't run to first base with any speed. It was a very hard thing to do, and Barry was horrible for the first few years, not making his father that happy with his success. As age and practice came along, Barry started to excel in doing things with his right arm. He realized he could hit the baseball farther and more accurately with his stronger left arm, pulling the swing. This accomplishment created a bond with his father and taught Barry the importance of trying, accepting change, and facing fears; after all, right is right.

Jacob enrolled Barry into boxing, and even though it is a sport that scared most young people, Barry enjoyed it. He learned very quickly why athletes who are left-handed normally do better in sports, as he excelled in boxing. Barry understood that with only 10% of humans being left-handed, right-handers struggle with the slim variety of training, whether it is soccer, football, or boxing. Perhaps being left-handed is a gift in sports and a gift in life.

Life around the ranch is always busy, so the family is very close, only leaving the ranch on special occasions. Most of those occasions are family-related, including weddings, reunions, or birthdays, where Barry gets to know his relatives. He enjoys his cousins, especially the boys, where he learns about mechanical things, hot rods, and just being a young man.

One uncle really strikes his attention; Jacob's youngest brother, Walter, who hasn't had a parent due to the loss of his parents at an early age. Walter seems to always be drinking, shooting guns, and fighting. Barry's father makes Walter go home on occasion to limit the crazy. Uncle Walter shows Barry what it means to be tough and perhaps a little crazy, crazy like Berserkers.

Uncle Walter had been away in the Army, so Barry didn't meet him until he returned from the war, when he started working for Jacob at the ranch. Barry learns to uphold values, be it his own or his family, even at the expense of self-injuries. It's a lesson that will stay with him for life: doing what's right, not just for himself, but for those who cannot defend themselves.

Family Bond

Barry grows up with his family, primarily closer to his sisters each day as they eat together, play together, and spend eight hours each day attending school together. This creates a lifelong bond—it has to—as talking and signs of affection are not something done in not part of Jacob's family ritual.

Living on a ranch or rural area, as one would expect, Barry and his sisters rode the bus to and from school each day. You make great friends on a bus ride, and you make some not-so-good friends also—that's just life. Jacob, like most fathers, wants to protect his family, especially his daughters, from the problems dealt to them by the outside world. Jacob expects Barry to fall in line, as he is the one closest to the girls most of the day.

One day after school, one of Barry's sisters was getting her hair pulled by the boy behind her in the back seat of the bus. Kids do things, and sometimes not always as bullying, but rather just to show some kind of interest. This is one of those times, and although it often escalates into something greater, perhaps there is no hatred involved. Kids learn these interactions by being kids—something they will not learn by being locked in a room at home.

The boy continues to pull her hair, irritating Barry's sister to the point where she turns around to punch the kid. The kid, trying to protect himself, ends up pushing her track cleats back into her face, punching four holes in her skin. Until that moment, it was something that Barry saw as harmless kid play, but now, as blood streamed down his sister's face, he reacted violently.

The bus driver stopped the bus, and Barry dragged the kid outside onto the road's edge, beating him up. Barry was ejected from the bus and had to run three miles home while his sisters remained on the bus.

When Barry got home, his mother was not happy with his actions, especially because the father of the boy who was beaten up was just pulling into the driveway. Barry's father was outside feeding the horses when he heard Barry's mother yelling for him to come to the house. At first, it was embarrassing to Jacob to hear about Barry's actions, but once he saw the face of his daughter, Jacob reacted, telling the boy's father to take his son and exit the ranch. Even though Jacob tells Barry not to do that kind of stuff on the bus, Barry can tell he's pleased that Barry protected his sister.

A few years later, at a school party, a boy calls Barry's sister a "bitch," and Barry throws the guy over a pool table and beats him up. Again, I think the boy liked Barry's sister, but when she rejected him, he struck out with an incorrect response.

Barry didn't really care about threats or ridicule thrown at him, but didn't like it when his group was being bullied for no reason. As time goes on, Barry sees less of his sisters, and after graduation, he moves away to college. At this point, he makes new friends in his college classes and during late-night shifts working as a mechanic.

Growing Up Fast

Barry attends CSB University that fall, and he sees things that he didn't deal with in early childhood on a ranch. Barry hadn't been around alcohol in his younger life, and that was a completely different game. He hadn't been around all types of young adults, especially girls, who are outgoing on their own.

Barry hangs around other college students who live in his dormitory hall, usually just hangs out in different kids' rooms or lifts weights with other gym rats. On occasion, Barry and his roommate drive to other towns to see the area and visit other colleges. Barry owns a fast car, and hot rods were very popular at that time. A lot of the time, other fast cars would seek out each other for a street race. Barry had been in many races and had a few tickets for drag racing against other cars; police knew about his car in the valley.

One evening, a young lady who was dating Barry's roommate needed a ride home just eight miles across town. Barry agreed to run her home with one condition—he didn't drive. Barry had consumed a few beers and wanted a friend of his to drive his car to eliminate the chances of getting pulled over by police.

Barry's friend was the only one who hadn't consumed alcohol for the evening, and being late at night made it harder to find someone else to hitch a ride. Barry's friend Anne was about the only person he trusted to drive his car. She was smart, honest, and didn't drink. Barry had known her since the first day of school and spent a lot of time with her.

Barry and Anne met each other in the registration line and hit it off, although both had steady girlfriends/ boyfriends. Barry had teased her for having orange hair, and he always called her 'Orangie.' Anne agreed, and they all loaded up to make the quick trip to run the female home, which was only a short 30-minute drive.

About halfway to the young lady's house, a police officer pulled Anne over in Barry's Trans Am, this being strange as they were doing nothing wrong. Anne was asked to get out of the car along with Barry, and the police officer noticed Anne was wearing flip-flops. The police officer asked why she was driving Barry's car, and Barry explained that they all had been drinking besides Anne. The officer informed Anne that it was illegal to wear flip-flops to operate a motor vehicle, even though Barry found it absurd.

Barry asked the officer how he could tell she wasn't wearing the correct shoes while she was driving down the road. The officer replied that she was driving a little slow for that kind of car. He informed Barry that they would have to impound the car unless someone with shoes was going to drive, and Barry agreed to drive, as he didn't want his car towed. The officer sent them on their way, with Barry driving and Anne riding shotgun in the Pontiac T/A. Barry went a couple of blocks, and the officer turned his lights on to pull them over again. Barry knew the reason, and it didn't feel right.

Barry started accelerating his car, and within a few moments, he lost the police car. Barry's car was extremely fast and reached a speed of 130 mph. Barry left the police in the dust and thought it would all be over as he reached the college campus. Unfortunately, the pursuing police had a roadblock set up with campus police. Barry pulled up to the roadblock, acting as if nothing was going on, although the campus police were pretty sure the description was correct, as a 1973 T/A was quite rare. The state police were in the area, so they got to the scene moments before the city police arrived to ID Barry and his car. The state police officer was very polite and realized there was probably more to the story than a drag-racing hot rod failing to yield. As the City officer pulled up to the scene, he exited his patrol car and slammed Barry over his trunek lid, punching him in the head.

The State police officer intervened and said he would pull seniority and handle the arrest; Barry could tell he saved him from a beating. Barry was arrested and charged with a DUI, while Anne was allowed to drive the car back to the college dormitory—with no shoes. Barry talked to the officer on the way, explaining what had happened. The officer responded, saying, "That doesn't seem right, but it's out of my hands."

Barry spent the night in jail and called his sister the next morning to bail him out, getting a lawyer a few days later. Barry's sister was in law school at the time and knew a lot of great lawyers, ultimately saving Barry's ass.

Barry faced charges of DUI, eluding an officer, and reckless driving in the coming months. Luckily, Barry's friend Anne had a great memory and was very smart—she remembered the first arresting officer's name, and with her testimony, all charges were dropped. The city police officer was reassigned to another job.

Before the day of court proceedings, Barry had Anne cut his hair—long hippie hair doesn't do well in a legal setting. He decides to go home to his parents for Thanksgiving. It's a long eight-hour drive, but he misses his family, especially his six-year-old younger brother.

On the drive down a curvy river road, Barry gets stuck behind a long line of cars traveling at only 20 MPH on a 60 MPH highway.

After following the slow-moving traffic for 10 to 15 miles, a straight passing zone finally appears. Barry seizes the opportunity, accelerating to 130 MPH and passing over 30 cars in one go. Just as he clears the last car, he spots a State Police vehicle barely a quarter mile ahead, coming toward him.

The officer immediately turns on his lights, and Barry knows he's about to get a ticket for speeding or reckless driving. Accepting his fate, he eases off the throttle and coasts to a safe pull-off area to wait. Slowly, the long line of cars he just passed crept by as Barry sat there, waiting for the officer.

When the officer pulls up beside Barry's car, he doesn't write a ticket—he just screams at him, warning him to never do that again. Without hesitation, Barry shouts back, "Yes, sir!" The officer then drives ahead and stops another car—an elderly man in a camper. As Barry pulls back onto the road, keeping to the speed limit, he sees the officer aggressively chewing out the 80-year-old driver. Barry doesn't stick around to find out whether the man gets a ticket for holding up traffic.

Barry decides that since winter is coming up, he will trade off the Pontiac T/A for a 4-wheel drive pickup, thinking it would be better for tickets and winter weather. Because of college costs, Barry works at a mechanic shop to make money and pay for college. His boss talks him into helping him out on weekends for some extra money, and he will give him a great deal on tires for his pickup. This includes going to races out of town to help with a Jeep dragster, driving long hours, and experiencing the world of racing. Barry learns a lot while attending races and enjoys talking to fellow racers about different ideas for engines and modifications. As winter approaches, Barry purchases tires for his pickup that his boss has promised him at a lower price and has saved the money needed to spend. Because of the money and his excitement to perform, Barry decides to buy a set of 40" Ground Hawg tires and install a lift kit on the truck to accommodate bigger tires. This really transforms Barry's truck into a very different vehicle. The truck was extremely tall and difficult to get into, as the doors were 3 feet from the ground.

One of the biggest problems with a vehicle of this lift was mud flaps, as the tires were out past the fenders of the truck and there was no protection from the rear. The second problem that made the vehicles more dangerous is the fact that the bumper height is 2-3 feet above any other vehicle on the road. Barry loves the truck, as do many friends around him, but he is not a favorite of the police; they notice it each time he drives by.

As if Barry's truck wasn't visible enough, he painted stripes and had it lettered, making it one in a million. The cops at the time didn't have much knowledge of what to do with these new types of vehicles. Until now, modifications were very limited because of price and limited technology, so information was slow to come. Barry had the advantage because of his involvement with racing and race products.

During the day, when things were busy, Barry and his truck were quite safe from getting pulled over, but come night, it was another thing. Low traffic, low police calls, and low-lying "stake-outs" always created a problem with Barry traveling around the city in the evening. Whether coming home from work, out on a date or attempting to return late from a hunting trip, it was always a battle with Barry's vehicle.

Barry works at a mechanics shop till 10 PM a lot of nights, loves hunting and shooting guns on his off days, and, of course, enjoys dating girls when he can.

On one occasion, Barry is on his way downtown after getting home from the gun range and gets pulled over by the police as he enters the city. Barry has been at the gun range with his friends, shooting and enjoying target practice with all their guns, both pistols and rifles. Barry pulls over and rolls down the window as the police officer starts off his spiel by asking for his driver's license and registration.

The officer checks out his vitals and returns to the vehicle, asking why he has spent brass all over his dash. Barry explains he had been shooting earlier that day. The officer asks Barry to exit his vehicle, which Barry agrees to, but while jumping down from the truck, the officer is too close to the door. Barry makes the jump, bumping into the door that the officer is holding, causing the officer to fall backwards onto the ground.

The officer freaks out. Even though it wasn't Barry's fault, no one could exit that vehicle with two feet of clearance without hurting their back on the door rocker panel. The officer pulls his weapon and tells Barry to get to the truck bedside, alerting dispatch that he needs more officers—all while still sitting on the asphalt from his fall. He informs Barry to put his hands on the bedside of the truck and spread his legs, which Barry complies with. The officer then gets up off the ground, puts his gun back into its holster, and informs Barry to freeze in that position. Barry kind of laughs.

This probably infuriates the officer, but the officer continues his job of frisking and searching Barry for any illegal products. Barry didn't do those types of activities, so it was never a concern of his to be searched, although he usually had derogatory things to say as it happened. Other officers begin to pull into the parking lot where Barry is, acting as though it was some big bust—possibly allowing them to receive some medals of honor.

The arresting officer was young and really upset, so another officer took charge and asked Barry what had happened. Barry responded that he had done absolutely nothing wrong and wasn't answering Jack Shit. This pissed off the officer, so he informed his fellow officers to handcuff and arrest Barry. Barry was then going to be an ass because at no point was it illegal to have empty shell cases in a vehicle without a motive.

Barry's truck bed was quite high. Barry easily reached it as he was 6'4" tall, although most of the officers struggled to reach it with any force. Barry was also extremely strong, and the officers couldn't get his arms off the bedside to apply handcuffs on him. After many attempts to release Barry's grip on the bedside, a couple of officers climbed into the truck bed, using their nightsticks to free Barry's hands. Barry was tough, but hitting fingers against metal with a baton hurts, no matter who you are, so Barry allowed the cops to cuff him.

Barry was arrested for resisting arrest. After a good chewing from the police captain that only makes it worse for himself, Barry is carried off in a police car. Barry's sister bails him out the next morning and retains a lawyer for him—once again, a favor he owes his family.

Weeks later, the police drop the charges of resisting arrest and serve him a ticket for No Mud Flaps! Barry pays the ticket to avoid the system of American courts.

Learning The Ropes

Barry thinks it's ridiculous that the police and American law are spending time on a few vehicles like this in the country, but nevertheless, he spends his own time studying the law as it affects him. Barry finds out that the law has a loophole in that both bumper height and mud flaps say nothing about the material that the "offense" can be made from. It just states the bumper must be within 8" from the highway and cover the outside of the tire, making Barry think! He welds a piece of small chain attached to his bumper, dropping down to 6" from the pavement. That way, it covers the law, doesn't make his truck look unattractive, and, the big reason, Barry won't get high-centered when out hunting.

Barry gets pulled over a few weeks later, as the cops feel he didn't learn his lesson. The officer is polite and just gives him a ticket for no mud flaps and too high of bumper height. The police know Barry and know they can't harass him, but feel they have him over a barrel, just where they want him. Either the police fine him to comply, or the vehicle gets impounded for compliance. Barry goes to court for the ticket a few weeks later, bringing all his pictures and a copy of the Idaho law. He shows all these items to the judge, telling him that he isn't trying to break the law, but that he has spent a lot of money on his truck to make it work for its intended purpose. The judge agrees with Barry and finds him not guilty, as the law is written. He informs

Barry that the law will probably get changed someday, but at present, it could be made from paper mâché and still conform with the law. The police officers attending the hearing are furious but have been told about the possibility of harassment charges, so they let it lay.

Barry's boss, Fred, loves fast cars, fast life, and fast times. He is a huge Ford enthusiast, owning a Ford F350 with duals on all four hubs, a Ford Mustang GT350, and a Kona jet boat with a 460 engine. He is very aggressive, very egotistical, and a great guy to be around if you want to have fun and live on the edge of death. Barry enjoys hanging out because Fred is an encyclopedia of knowledge and can make a boring day crazy. Barry does a lot of things with Fred, including building engines, attending races, and going to the bar occasionally. Fred has a reputation for being loud, obnoxious, and fighting, which doesn't go well with most of the patrons, in town or in the bars. Barry feels that because Fred was a helicopter pilot in Vietnam, he was trained to live on the edge. If a fight breaks out, it's usually Fred talking smack with somebody, but Barry still sticks up for his boss and enters the fight on his side.

The thing Barry loves most is going out on Fred's boat, as he has never been in a speed boat before. His youth allows him to go fishing and water skiing on small boats but never fly across the water at 80 MPH. Barry loves the fact that you can fly across the water, do anything you want, and never have to worry about the law. On a weekend outing, Barry is riding in Fred's boat, speeding down the river, when Barry notices the boat's fuel gauge says empty, so he yells at Fred to alert him. Fred laughs and says that POS is never correct, and at that very moment, the engine sputters and dies, causing the boat to lose its steering. The boat slowly turns toward the rock levee, still traveling at a high rate of speed, and starts to climb the large rocks along the bank. The boat climbs higher and higher, almost flipping upside down, until it slides back into the water when its speed is reduced to nothing. The boat sinks in the water a few minutes later from large gouges in the bottom of the hull from the rocks. The party is over, as the boat has to be retrieved with Fred's winch and transported back to the shop.

The next few weeks are spent disassembling the boat, including pulling the engine and stripping everything off the boat to make the repairs. Barry enjoys learning how that procedure takes place, so he helps as much as he can in restoring Fred's boat. He learns the crazy world of fiberglass and gelcoat, which he never knew existed in the "body and fender" world. After just a few weeks, the boat is fixed, has a fresh new coat of paint, and is ready for the water! That weekend, Fred and Barry hit the water again, even though people tell Barry that if he hangs out with Fred, someday he will probably die. Fred has been a helicopter pilot in Vietnam and is no stranger to death. His daily routine seems to still be living on the edge, all the way up to the 20 piranhas he has in his house aquarium.

Barry goes one weekend with Fred when a couple of other jet boats are in the park, which is all you need to work up Fred for a duel. Fred and Barry start speeding toward the huge dam wall, concrete towering hundreds of feet, holding millions of gallons of water in the reservoir. The object is to see how high up the concrete wall with the jet spray they can get, and the winner will be awarded. The driver needs to drive toward the wall as fast as possible and flip the boat backward by pulling the Jetivator, spraying the wall. Fred does this numerous times when a universal joint decides to fail, causing the engine to overrev and the pump to stop working. The boat is traveling 60 MPH backward when it smashes into the concrete wall, causing the boat to break in half right in front of the engine compartment. Fred and Barry are thrown backward into the water. Barry is still sitting in the seat when it strikes the wall, and Barry uses the seat cushion to float as the engine and boat sink out of sight. It's a bad day for Fred, and a huge cost to him, as he must pay divers to retrieve his boat from the bottom of the river in the days to come.

This drives Barry's desire to buy a boat for himself even higher than it has been all year. Barry drives to a boat manufacturer the next weekend to look at and test-drive new boats. He loves the hundreds of boats they have for sale, test-driving 4-5 different ones, and decides on a bright orange Tahiti 19' boat, which is more his style. It's a Chevy!

Barry loves his new boat and loves to waterski, not only because it's fun for him but because it's a great way to meet new friends. Barry graduates from college that fall semester and stops working for Fred as he starts his own career, although he keeps in touch with Fred for many years. Barry has summers off and is done teaching at 4 o'clock each day, allowing him to get to the lake most of the warm seasons. The community has a boat group, SIBA, made up of local boaters who do yearly cleanups and sign painting at the local marinas, which Barry joins. Barry volunteers to clean up the marina he is closest to and enjoys the most for waterskiing. Barry contacts a few people to help: one is a friend of his who owns a dozer, his uncle who owns a backhoe, and some boat owners for manual labor. They prepare a landing area for launching, a small parking lot for guests, and, most importantly, a beach free of trash and noxious weeds. It isn't perfect but is a start to make the area into an enjoyable boating experience. Barry receives a lot of compliments and is happy that what he does helps owners avoid damaging their boats and injuring skiers.

After a couple of months, the city votes to start charging visitors coming into the park to cover upkeep and maintenance. This is new to the public, and for boaters, it is against the law. The park was donated to the city by a woman who wanted it to remain free to the public. The city gets around this by stating it's for maintenance and not a charge for the park itself. Unfortunately, the boat ramp is only accessible by driving through the park. The fee is small, only $2.00 per trip, and for most people, it's not a big deal, but for Barry, it adds up to hundreds of dollars a year. Most importantly, it's illegal. Barry pays the fee a few times, thinking it's just a one-time thing, but then starts driving past the attendants, refusing to pay. The first time or so, the attendant just lets it go, but after the first couple of times, they call the police. The police respond to the boat launch, asking Barry what's going on with his failure to pay the fee. Barry tells the officers that the boat launch is owned by the IF&G, that the city constitution states there can be no charge to access the park, and even if it were legal, Barry didn't use the park. The police don't really know what to do but give Barry a ticket for trespassing, allowing a judge to decide. Barry doesn't like the fact that he is guilty before the jurisdiction is read but figures it's the police officers' way of not getting in the middle.

Barry prints out all the necessary paperwork as he goes to court a few days later, preparing for his defense of trespassing. The judge dismisses the case and instructs the city director of parks and rec to solve the problem by just giving season passes to boat owners and stop involving young employees to police the problem. Barry is happy about the decision, and even though he receives a park pass in the mail a few days later, Chad from P&R isn't all that pleased with the judge's decision.

As the summer season progresses, Barry tries to make the beach nicer to spend the day by bringing a truckload of sand and acquiring a few old picnic tables for boaters to sit on. Barry calls the state marine tax department to ask questions about acquiring some docks for boaters to use for tying up boats when they're not in use. Barry gets ahold of a man who is very helpful and brilliant at his job, something Barry wasn't expecting to find on any phone call, let alone the first one. Barry explains he is a member of the boater's club and has been fixing up the launch area, hoping to get a few docks for the marina. The tax official states that there should be 7 docks there, and the rotation for 2 new docks will be available the next year. Barry responds that there are no docks. The official is very concerned about the whereabouts of the docks and asks Barry if he would be available to meet him at the marina the following Tuesday. Barry informs him he can meet any time to look at what they have done at the marina and would help him try to solve the problem. The official states he would like to meet Barry at 10 o'clock AM for about an hour but doesn't want him around when he meets with Parks & Rec at 11 o'clock that day. Barry meets with the tax official at 10 o'clock, shows him some of the new improvements, and then they part ways, although the tax official guarantees Barry that he will receive 2 new docks the next week. Barry never knows the complete process that went on that day; he only hears secondhand information, but it wasn't a good day for Chad at P&R. Chad is kind enough to leave a message on Barry's answering machine about how much he hates him.

Barry decides to go to another reservoir and marina that next weekend with some of his friends for a change of venue, letting things cool down a little at the local park. They decide to go to Lucky Peak and spend the night in a motel so they can water ski for the entire weekend. They drive up early Saturday and get to the lake by 10 o'clock AM, launch the boat, and enjoy a day of skiing until about 5 PM. At that time, they decide to go back into town, get dinner, and hit the local bars to dance and meet new people. Barry and his friends move around town, bar-hopping, checking out the large town nightlife, hooking up with some girls at one of the dance clubs. Barry is tired, so by the time midnight rolls around, he tells his friends he's heading to the motel. His friends aren't quite ready to leave, so they stay behind. His friends tell him they will catch a cab to the motel after the bar closes, but one young lady decides to ride with Barry back to the motel. As Barry drives his pickup and boat from the bar downtown to the motel, he's tired and really doesn't pay attention to his speed. An officer flashes his lights and pulls behind him, signaling him to pull over. Barry pulls over in the exact motel parking lot he's staying at and parks in one of the spots. The officers approach the vehicle on each side of Barry's truck and ask for his driver's license and registration. Barry obliges, handing over the appropriate items, and asks why he got pulled over, thinking perhaps the lights on his trailer aren't working. The officer says he clocked him at 42 MPH in a 35 MPH zone, so he's getting a ticket for speeding. Barry smiles and jokes about being in the parking lot of the motel he's staying at, so he couldn't have been speeding for more than a couple hundred feet. The officer then asks the girl for her driver's license, and she states she doesn't have an ID but that her name is Lisa. The officers say they will need her birthdate to confirm her ID, which makes her very anxious to provide anything. This pisses the officers off and they inform both Barry and Lisa to exit the vehicle, at which time they shine their flashlights in the truck and see Barry's .45 handguns under the seat. The officers freak out and inform both of them to put their hands on the hood, which they do. Barry tries to inform the police that it's no big deal; we're in Idaho, everybody has a gun in their truck, and they're not LAPD. This enrages the officers even more, cuffing Barry and putting him in the back of the patrol car, charging Barry with a concealed firearm. Barry is tired and really hopes they're just being difficult, as Barry doesn't want to escalate this more than just a speeding ticket. Lisa is crying by this time and asking the police to please let her go, as she just met Barry an hour before. They decline, and once they get feedback from dispatch, they find out she has a felony for drug possession from years earlier. They call for backup but feel it's an officer's duty to frisk the person for weapons or drugs, so they proceed with that task. They pat her up and down her torso and then bend her over the vehicle, lifting her miniskirt and looking inside her panties for drugs. Lisa screams and cries, and Barry feels the officers went too far without a female officer and a room present, so he reacts.

Both officers are paying attention to the task at hand when Barry kicks the rear door window out of the police car and exits the vehicle. The police car is way behind Barry's hood, as his truck and boat are very long. Neither officer hears the glass breaking due to road noise and the distance. Barry is really pissed and runs toward the officers at the front of his truck. Barry hadn't been noticed, which completely caught the officers off guard as he approached. When Barry reaches the officers, one of them faces Barry, amazed that he's out of the car and still in cuffs. Barry knows he can't fight in cuffs, so he does what he can and kicks the officer between the legs as hard as he can. The officer goes down onto the ground, and Barry jumps on him, headbutting him in the face until the other officer jumps in to break up the fight. Barry is a lot stronger than the two officers, and they struggle to keep Barry from headbutting the one on the ground. At that moment, the backup officers pull up on the scene, and they pull shotguns on Barry, demanding he stop what he's doing. Barry complies, and they take him to the precinct, where he is booked into jail. Barry is still pissed about the treatment from the police and tells the captain he needs his high blood pressure pills before morning. The captain asks EMS to check his readings. EMS personnel freak out that his blood pressure is that high, so they recommend they keep a watchful eye on him the rest of the night. Barry gets to sleep in the office while Lisa must dress down into an orange jumpsuit and gets put into a jail cell.

Barry waits until his sister answers the phone in the morning. She hires an attorney to show up at the jail on a Sunday to bail both Barry and Lisa out and gives them a ride to the motel. Barry's sister has retained the attorney to represent both him and Lisa in court. He is a great attorney. As they pull into the parking lot of the motel at 8 o'clock in the morning, they see Barry's interior truck parts all over the lot. The police have stripped the interior out of his truck looking for drugs. Barry's lawyer takes pictures with his camera, instructing Barry to do what he can to put the truck back together for the day and let him handle the legal matter. Barry does just that, and then he goes inside the motel and wrestles his friends out of bed to have breakfast and hit the lake for a day of waterskiing.

Barry goes back home that night and waits for a couple of weeks for his attorney to call about going to court. The day comes, and Barry drives back to Boise to attend court with his attorney. Barry is amazed by his attorney as the court carries on; he doesn't miss anything with the two officers, and after it's over, Lisa's charges are dismissed, and Barry only has to pay for the speeding ticket. Barry's attorney returns the two Colt .45s to Barry that were confiscated by the police, and just like his truck, the guns have been stripped—no barrels, no grips—and Barry isn't happy. Barry's attorney explains that he thinks it's illegal, but at this time, just count your blessings and walk away, as his fees would cost more than the parts that are missing. Barry agrees with his attorney and tells him that the police officer he had headbutted will need the money to get his nose fixed anyway.

Barry decides to sell his boat and get some jet skis. He buys two new Kawasaki 550 stand-ups, one for himself and one for any friend that wants to go. Barry rides them during the year but realizes it is best to keep just one, as the extra one just seems to get wrecked a lot by inexperienced operators, so he decides to sell one. Barry goes to a dealer in the area, and they tell him they will give him the brand-new spring edition if he trades in the two older ones. Barry decides that's the best option, and he'll enjoy the new, improved ski. He goes into the courthouse a few days later and attempts to register the new jet ski. The woman working the window asks Barry how much he paid for it, and Barry responds, "Nothing, I traded in some other jet skis." The woman says that he will have to pay sales tax on the value of the boat. So, what might that be? Barry says he's already paid sales tax on the old ones, so their value would be the same. Barry laughs and says, "That's the reason we, as Americans, poured tea into the harbor." Barry walks out of the DMV without registering the ski.

Barry decides to use the ski without registering it for the summer. Barry goes to a lake with a friend the next weekend and puts the jet ski in the water. He borrows his friend's pickup as his truck is hooked to his fifth-wheel camper. He goes out on the lake for a couple of hours, and then he gets pulled over by the water police. They ask where his sticker is for registration, and Barry tells them he tried to get one, but the lady wouldn't sell him one. They say that's no excuse, so they're going to have to issue him a $500 ticket. Barry just drives off, going to the other side of the lake. After about 20 minutes, the police boat comes over to where he's playing in a cove. They signal him to pull over, but Barry just ignores them and heads to the other side of the lake where his trailer is. As Barry is driving off with the jet ski and trailer, the police are pulling into the boat ramp. Barry just drives off as the police write down the license plate on his friend's truck. A few weeks later, Barry's friend receives a ticket in the mail and calls the courthouse, stating that he doesn't own a jet ski. They drop the charges. Barry sells his ski later that fall.

On His Own

Barry's shop is going very well with his knowledge of engine building and understanding the values of torque on big engines. His shop is building high-torque engines for pullers and some street cars, getting his name out there in the livestock community, where power is everything on long hauls and steep hills. Barry has a lot of clients in construction and ranching who use large trailers for hauling things that need more power. One weekend, while Barry is at home, a friend of his brings a car by his house to look at as he is struggling with making it run correctly. Barry tells the owner that he can fix it, so the car is unloaded off the trailer and into his garage.

Barry loves racing and has learned a bunch from his old boss and other smart mechanics. Barry learns at an early age that learning from very smart people is invaluable in life. He understands that most smart people will gift knowledge to people with an attitude to learn. He knows that people, but especially successful people, love to help those who will take that gift of life and use it. Barry doesn't specialize in racing at his shop, as he knows there is no stable money in it for him. Every mechanic dreams of racing in some sort or another, but has to expect the reality of just perfecting their business to success.

The owner of the car is a young female racer, who got directed to Barry by community people about his love for Chevrolet. Her name is Terry, and she is new to racing and has a little money for the sport.

Terry's car is a 1969 Chevelle with a 454 BB engine in it. It's a great fit for Barry, given his many engine builds over the last 8 years working with this setup. Barry has grown up in the age of Big Block muscle cars, sharpening his teeth with performance engines. Barry talks to Terry, trying to find out what she is wanting to achieve with her racing project. They decide on changing a few parts, but mostly the setup just needs adjusting and fine-tuning. Terry explains that she was hoping to attend a race in Boise that weekend, and Barry tells her that would happen. Terry really likes Barry, his humor, and his attention to perfection. She tells one of Barry's friends that he is the only mechanic she has known who washes his hands every 5 minutes. Barry gets the car ready and tells Terry he will run over with her to help adjust the car for the weekend. That pleases Terry, as she is a driver, not a mechanic.

Barry and Terry get the car to the racetrack, and the car runs very well for a full-body race car. Terry is happy with the way the car runs and asks Barry that if he would continue to help her, she would pay his way to the races. Barry agrees, both because of his love for racing and the fact that he is making money doing it. Barry decides to close his shop on Fridays so that he can attend races out of state. At one of the races, Terry explodes the driveline out of the car, shoving the driveline into the floor pan. It scares Terry, but all the other racers tell her that at least she knows her motor is producing a lot of horsepower. The two of them go to 8-9 races before the season ends. Terry wins a few races and gets in the top ten the rest, making her ecstatic to race the next year.

During the winter, Terry decides to move out of a modified streetcar and into an actual race car. Barry and she drive to Las Vegas and purchase a 67 Corvette BB funny car. On the way back to Idaho, she asks Barry if he would close his shop and be her full-time mechanic. Barry tells her he would think about it and let her know in a few days. The next week, Terry calls him to run to lunch for an hour or so, and Barry agrees. They go grab burgers to go for lunch, and Terry drives over to an auto dealership that had gone out of business a few years back. She has purchased it and tells Barry he can have the entire shop to build cars if he races with her full-time. Barry agrees, as he can't see any reason not to. The shop is 4 times bigger than his, and he will have no expenses.

The race is on, and Terry purchases a new dually pickup, a new enclosed trailer, and Barry gets the car ready for spring races. Barry and Terry travel all over the West racing and having a good time vacationing along the way. Barry loves the experience and gets the opportunity to meet famous people and builders, giving him a lot of knowledge and contacts. Barry still has time to build engines for other people and work on his own custom cars. Barry spends a lot of time and money on his 70 Corvette with a 496 BB. Towards the end of the race season, Terry starts to seem upset and colder in her day-to-day interactions. She tells Barry one day she can't pay him, but he is welcome to stay in the shop and make money. It's a little disturbing, but Barry starts advertising for clients like the old days.

Barry is not sure what the problem is. He's tried to ask, but Terry doesn't want to talk about anything. Barry notices that on occasion, she will be crying in her office. Barry starts bouncing in a local bar to make extra money, and one night she stops by the bar to tell him she is going on vacation for a couple of months to get away for a while. She leaves town with her boyfriend, and Barry doesn't see her again for a year.

A few weeks go by, and Barry is at the shop working when some police officers and FBI agents pull into the shop. They come inside and start asking a few questions about everything in the shop, then tell

Barry he will be kicked out of the shop and that they will seize everything in sight. Barry argues with them about seizing his livelihood, his checking account, but they don't care. All the doors of the shop are locked with chains, and police tape is everywhere. Barry doesn't even have money until he gets paid from bouncing at the bar in a couple of days. Barry ends up working for a friend for a couple of months to have enough money to live on, make house payments, and at least function. The FBI, meanwhile, is questioning Barry every other day about where Terry is hiding, where the money went, and what type of things they purchased. Barry doesn't know about these things to start with but pleads the 5th on everything they ask. He mainly treats them poorly, as they don't care about his livelihood, and he doesn't care about theirs. The FBI officers tell him one day he's the biggest A-hole they have ever met. Five months later, they allow him to go into the shop and recover his tools and parts that are his. Barry rents another shop with a friend of his and starts all over. This time, he hopes not to get caught up in any BS. The FBI tracks down Terry a few months later, arrests, convicts, and sentences her to 5 years in prison. She informs the officers that while she loved Barry's trust and companionship, he has nothing to do with her money issues and fraud.

Come winter, Barry is getting busy at his new shop and has a customer come in wanting his pickup engine rebuilt. The man is older and a character with a lot of war stories from Africa years ago. He tells Barry and the shop employees that the pickup was with him in Africa while he was stationed there. Barry agrees to do the work and gives him an estimate for $6,800, which the man agrees to pay. The gentleman stops by from time to time to check on progress, and after a month, the pickup is ready to go. The man stops by to check on his vehicle and wants to go for a test drive once it is finished. Barry tells him that would be fine, but he will have to ride along for security. The man agrees, and they proceed to test drive the truck for a few miles, then return to the shop very happy with the performance of the new engine. The man states that he will return to the shop the next day to retrieve the pickup truck. Barry tells him that would be fine and that they are open until 6:00 PM. However, if he's running late, just give him a call, and Barry will stay late.

The next morning, when Barry arrives at the shop, the first thing he notices is that the truck is missing. He calls the owner to see if he has picked it up, and the owner explains to him that he took it in the middle of the night. Barry asks if he is stopping by with a check later that day, and the man informs him that he will not be paying for it. Barry asks why, and the man states he doesn't have the money to pay for the pickup but thanks him for the work. Barry is bewildered and pissed, so he calls the police. They inform him it's a civil matter and out of their hands. Barry checks the man's address on his work order and, after work, drives to the address outside of town, finding the truck parked in a shed near the house. Barry approaches the truck, and he hears someone scream from the house that they have called the police. Barry has the keys to start and drive off the truck, but figures it would be better to just wait for the police to arrive.

Within a few minutes, a police car pulls in and asks what the problem is. Barry explains the situation and tells him he is taking the truck until payment is made. The officer says the vehicle is on private property, and taking it would get him charged with grand theft, so it's best that he leaves. The officer tells him that if it was on public property and the man wasn't around, things would be different, and Barry would have the right to take it. A few days later, one of Barry's friends calls him and tells him the vehicle is at the courthouse in town, and the owner is not with the vehicle. Barry jumps in his truck and drives over to the courthouse parking lot, pulling up beside the pickup truck in question and parking. Just as Barry gets out, the owner of the vehicle comes out, spots them, and runs back inside to get police help. The sheriff comes out and explains to Barry that he has no authority to tow the vehicle until he goes to court and gets a judgment. Barry is angry and tells both the owner and the sheriff his feelings on stealing from him to the point that not only is every window at the 3-story courthouse open, but the sheriff tells him if he doesn't leave, he will be arrested. Barry yells a few choice words at the cops and then drives off, telling the sheriff he will be back to file a lien.

A few days later, Barry gets all the paperwork needed to file a lawsuit against the truck owner, hoping to get a lien and recover his money. Barry and the pickup truck owner show up for court and wait their turn to give their side of the story. Barry goes first and explains the story to the judge, hoping to win the case. Barry doesn't see how he could lose. The owner of the truck goes next and explains to the judge that his truck is better than it was new and how great of a mechanic Barry is. Both the judge and Barry are confused as to why he would just accuse himself of the crime by admitting his guilt like that. The judge tells both Barry and the truck owner that he has no choice but to award a judgment to Barry for the full amount of the lien. At that time, the truck owner approaches the bench, hands a piece of paper to the judge, and stands back as it's being read. The judge has a strange look on his face as he reads through the paper, turns to Barry, and tells him he will check with authorities to double-check the paper content, but cannot enter judgment at that time. A few days later, Barry receives a letter from the judge explaining that the man is a veteran of the U.S. Army and is not responsible to pay the bill. Barry wonders what kind of country sets up a law that causes business owners to be responsible for veterans' bills. Barry writes it off as a business loss, although Barry does run into the truck owner in a grocery store a few weeks later and has some words with him, causing the man to fall on the floor and scream bloody murder. Barry realizes the man has some problems, and being a veteran doesn't explain it.

Barry learns his business cannot take losses like this, so he will have to tighten his ship with future customers. He tells his employees to be careful on test drives and not leave finished vehicles outside after business hours. Barry has one vehicle that has been inside the shop for over a year, sitting in one corner taking up needed room. Barry pulls it outside and puts a couple of covers on it to protect it from the weather. It doesn't even look like a car with all the covers and tarps, so Barry feels good about leaving it there, especially with other items parked in front of it. The owner of the vehicle has gone through a divorce and has no contact information, but Barry has known him for years and figures he will come get his car someday. Barry and his wife go on a vacation for a few days, and when they return, the car is gone from the parking lot. Barry goes to court to get the car or the money granted to him and wins his $14,000 owed. Unfortunately, both the car and the owner have vanished. Barry asks the city police if they knew whether they had noticed the license plate of the tow vehicle. Their response is that they only saw it getting loaded but didn't pay attention to who was doing it, even though it was on a Sunday. Barry wonders how many businesses closed on Sundays would not get questioned about loading up things. Barry knows he won't get his money in his lifetime.

During the winter, Barry drives his backhoe between the shop and his personal house to do snow removal, using the highway. Barry's backhoe can only travel approximately 20 MPH, so Barry has purchased a slow-moving vehicle sign to put on the rear so that he will be legal. One day, a policeman pulls him over on the highway for blocking traffic during one of Barry's trips. He informs Barry that he cannot be on the highway going 20 MPH, holding up traffic. Barry tells the officer that the emblem on the rear is why he can do it, and it's only for a half-mile stretch, causing the officer to get upset about Barry's denial to accept the law. He then asks Barry for his ID, as he is giving him a ticket for driving equipment on a state highway. Barry informs him that not only can he be on the highway, but also doesn't need a driver's license to operate heavy equipment anywhere. The officer calls dispatch to bring a tow truck and additional officers to remove Barry and his backhoe. Dispatch tells him to let Barry go, as he has the right of way. Barry's friend from the gym tells Barry that the police had played the recording of the incident at a police training to show officers how NOT to handle any situation. Barry laughs and states he feels honored to be able to help in educating police officers.

Barry has started dating a young woman who has a daughter from a previous marriage. The young girl is only 9 months old, and Barry gets quite close with her while they are dating. After a year or so, Barry finds out that the woman is pregnant, so they decide to get married. In the next few months, while the two are planning the wedding, the now 2-year-old has an accident. She is crushed by a swing set at the daycare and needs surgery on her arm. Her mother has insurance from working at Sears, but that insurance is denied because it happened at a business. A lawsuit against the daycare is successful, but unfortunately, the daycare has no business insurance and files for bankruptcy. It's understandable, as the woman would have lost her house if she hadn't filed for protection, but it still leaves a bill of $30,000 to be paid. Barry's girlfriend has no job and no real assets, so the bill and its lien go dormant. Barry is young and doesn't know that the lien will follow him someday. Barry gets married a few months later and welcomes a son into the family. In a stroke of luck, Barry keeps most of his things in his shop because of room at his small house. One evening, the police stop by and have judgment liens to pick up a lot of Barry's things. Luckily, the cops find nothing there and retreat for the night. The next day, Barry puts all his valuables in his sister's name, except for his house. By the time the credit bureau gets things lined out, the only thing they can attach a lien to is his house. Barry sells his house and moves on, starting over with a place to live. Between money, jobs, and arguing, Barry and his new wife struggle with being married after a few years, and they decide to go their separate ways.

After Barry's divorce, his ex-wife moves back home to her parents while Barry is forced to find an apartment. It's a small apartment located over a two-car garage, but it's cheap, and Barry likes that. He's very busy, so he doesn't care about a large house, just a place to lay his head. Barry lives in the apartment for about 9 months, and then the police stop by and inform him that the place is condemned and he must move out. He informs the police that he has his son for Christmas vacation, and hell and high water would make him leave before January. The cops murmur a few words but tell Barry they'll try to close their eyes for a couple of weeks. They know Barry and understand that it's Christmas, and getting evicted four days before Christmas day sucks. Barry's landlord calls him and tells him he must move out in 24 hours, or he will get fined $500 a day. Barry tells him the same thing as he told the cops, and the landlord is really upset with Barry. He informs him that he is an attorney and will prosecute Barry to the limits of the law. Barry laughs and tells the landlord he will move on January 2 when he takes his son back home from his break. Barry returns his son to his ex-wife and moves into a motel on the promised date. Barry calls the landlord the next day and asks when he can pick up his $500 deposit. The landlord informs Barry he will not be getting his deposit back as he didn't move out when requested. Barry tries to reason with him, stating that he was the one who was inconvenienced, as he had a one-year lease.

Barry files a lawsuit in small claims court, not for the money, but for the fact that it wasn't right. Come court day, the landlord doesn't appear for the lawsuit proceedings, and Barry is awarded his $500, plus court fees. Barry is happy. Before the 30-day waiting period is over, Barry gets a notice in the mail that the case will be appealed; he'll need to reappear again for court. Barry had told the judge the day of the first proceedings that lawyers always get special treatment, whereas a normal guy would have been issued a warrant for his arrest. The judge scolded Barry about special treatment in his court for attorneys, and the judge remembers the discussion as Barry walks into the courtroom. Barry states his case again and adds that now he has had to take two days off for the same case. The judge then turns to the defendant, Barry's landlord, and asks him to state his defense. When finished, Barry's landlord states he is countersuing for the fines he received.

The judge gives a stern lecture to Barry's landlord and tells him that he gives attorneys a bad name for his actions in and out of the courtroom. Barry is astonished when the judge starts listing out his awarded money, one by one. Barry gets his deposit money, moving fees, and his motel paid for 30 days to find a place to live, and 2 days of paid leave. The attorney is beyond furious and tells Barry he will never pay him a dollar as long as he lives. Barry must wait another 30 days for an appeal from district court, which he thinks the landlord will do to get a new judge. The 30 days come and go, and now Barry must figure out how to get his money. Barry asks his older sister, the attorney, how he could get money from someone who refuses to pay. She directs him to take his court judgment and go to the police department, allowing them to collect the cash. Barry does that, and the sheriff instructs him to meet him at a restaurant owned by the attorney at 6:00 PM. Barry goes to the restaurant at 5:55 PM, and the sheriff comes out with the cash Barry is to receive. It's a good day for Barry, but he hears the landlord is upset with the police department.

Sometimes, the law works in this country, and Barry is always happy to see when it happens.

On a late winter night, Barry is trying to clear his parking lot from snow. It has snowed over a foot, and his shop will open in 3 hours. He is moving back and forth with the loader, not much to see at 5 AM in the dark, pushing snow into a pile. After plowing snow for over an hour, Barry sees a car pull up in front of him, trying to drive around the shop to get to the convenience store on the other side. The driver just freezes as she realizes a huge loader is traveling around the backside of the building. Barry slams on the brakes, but with the slick, snowy surface, the 15,000-pound loader can't stop fast enough to prevent hitting the car. The loader hits the passenger side of the car and bends the Subaru so severely that none of the doors will open. The young lady must exit the vehicle through a side door window. She is furious and blames Barry for not stopping in time, stating that she just purchased the car 4 days earlier. Barry apologizes to her, stating that he didn't think anyone would be cutting through his lot at 5 AM and pulling in front of snow removal equipment. She hysterically calls 911 and demands a police officer come arrest Barry. While waiting, she walks around the new car for damage. Barry knows cars, and he knows the car will be totaled due to the severe damage to the frame.

The police arrive and start asking questions about how the wreck happened. The woman is still screaming that her brother-in-law is Bill Paxton, a famous movie star, and her husband, Steve, will kick Barry's ass. The police then ask the woman if Barry had those flashing lights on the loader and if she saw the yellow flash before she even saw the loader. She answers yes, and at that time, the officer hands her a ticket for "failure to yield to snow removal equipment," making her lose her mind. She screams at Barry, and Barry tries to tell her he knows her husband very well and that he goes snowmobiling with him every now and then. She calls her husband, and Barry knows his relationship with Steve will never be the same, but Barry feels good about the relationship with the law.

That next spring, Barry is at home on a Sunday when 3 of his friends come by and ask him to run out on a warm spring day to shoot rock chucks. Barry doesn't really want to go, but his friends are relentless, as he's been just working all the time. They load up in Dirk's truck, and Barry, Randy, and Curtis get in with their guns and ammo. They drive down by the canyon rim, stop the pickup, and unload themselves and the guns. They decide to walk a couple of miles along the canyon, look for rock chucks, and shoot as many as they can. After walking for a couple of hours, they don't see any animals, as it's just too early and the weather is cool for spring. They decide to walk back to the truck, and on the way back, they stop and shoot at some rocks and tree stumps, not giving much thought about hunting critters. Once they get close to the truck, they notice another vehicle parked beside it, and they wonder what it's doing so close to Dirk's truck. As they near the vehicle, a man gets out, and they realize it is an officer from Fish and Game. The officer seems upset at just some young guys out walking and shooting at rocks and informs them to hand over their hunting licenses. They all admit they hadn't even thought about getting licenses for the year, and it was just a spur-of-the-moment thing. He says they are all receiving a ticket for "failure to carry a license," and he is going to have to confiscate their guns. Barry shouts that it's stupid to get a ticket, but that his father had given him the gun he had in his possession, and nobody is taking the gun. The officer becomes very aggressive about dropping their guns, drawing his pistol, and demanding they do what he says. The other three men drop their guns, but Barry tells the officer that he doesn't

37

think he has the balls to shoot him in the back, and Barry starts running towards home. The officer yells for Barry to stop, but Barry just starts singing Army chant songs, "I don't know, but I've been told," as Barry is getting farther away. The officer continues to yell a bunch of times, but Barry just runs the 8 miles home. He's not losing another gun to the police.

A couple of months go by, and Barry hasn't even talked to his friends. He thought perhaps it had all blown over, and the officer had just let it slide. That was not the case. Barry's friends had been in jail for a sentence of 6 months because of forging a hunting license at a local sporting goods store. Once the officer had taken care of the men in jail, he set his sights on Barry. Strangely enough, Barry is playing tennis with a friend when a man comes up to him and asks if he is Barry. As soon as Barry turns around and sees the uniform, he knows who it is, and the guy has already drawn his gun. It would be difficult to run inside a chain-link fence with cuffs; Barry is going to jail. Barry knows he is in deep trouble but nevertheless asks the officer if he will need to confiscate his tennis racket, after all, it's a Wilson. The officer doesn't answer, but Barry knows the officer hates him. Barry then asks if he can go put some clothes on in his truck. The officer allows him to put on a shirt.

Once at the courthouse, the judge has agreed to arraign Barry since it's only 2:00 PM, and it's possible that Barry can bail out that day. The officer doesn't like that, as he hates Barry for his stunt months ago and wants to see him in jail. The judge hears the case and realizes Barry has a shop to tend to, and lets him go without bail, setting a court date for the next week. The next week, Barry goes to court, and the judge asks Barry about the case. After a few incident questions, the judge asks Barry if he is related to Brenda. Brenda is Barry's sister and an attorney in Washington, and Barry explains to the judge that it's his sister. The judge tells Barry that Brenda is the smartest woman he's ever met and that if anything had rubbed off, Barry couldn't be all bad. Judge Shaud fines Barry $75 plus court costs and tells him not to ever come back. Barry agrees and pays the money.

Barry decides to take some time off and run up to watch a Vandal game in Moscow. While at the game, he runs into some old friends, and they decide to run to Coeur d'Alene for some drinks and fun. When they arrive at the local bar, it's packed after the game, hardly a space to stand, let alone sit. About that time, the ladies' bathroom floods and must be closed for the evening for repairs. The bouncer lets guys and girls use the men's bathroom by alternating between two girls and two guys. As you can imagine, the line backs up all the way to Topeka, KS, and Barry walks outside to find a place in the back of the parking lot. Barry knows he should probably drive somewhere to use another restroom, but he didn't drive to the bar with his car. Barry walks to the back of the parking lot, between two cars, and starts to urinate in the dark when an officer grabs his arm. The officer tells him to finish his business and put his arms behind his back, as he's under arrest. Barry tells him it's impossible to have 400 people in a bar, drinking, and not having bathrooms available, so the bar should be the one arrested. The officer doesn't take any of his bull and escorts him down to the local precinct, charging him with "urinating in a public parking lot." Barry's friends must come down the next morning to bail him out, and they drive home to Southern Idaho.

Barry must drive all the way back up to Northern Idaho two weeks later to face the judge, not even knowing what penalty he will receive. Barry walks into court, sits down, and waits until his name is called. After about 30 minutes, the clerk calls his name. Barry stands up to affirm he's there, at which time the girl, chuckling a little, states, "You are being charged with urinating in a public parking lot." The judge asks what happened, and Barry tells his story, hoping to convince him that it wasn't his fault. The judge doesn't seem to care about his excuse and says to Barry, "This will be the most expensive piss you'll ever take," and charges him $200. The courtroom laughs out loud, and Barry, facing embarrassment, leaves the courtroom.

On the way home, Barry is driving alone late at night after a 9-hour drive, not really keeping an eye on his speed, and gets pulled over. He knows he was speeding, but he sees his Colt .45 lying on the floor and knows that it's not good. As the officer starts walking up to the side of Barry's truck, Barry thinks he should slide the gun under his seat but feels it will look like he's guilty of hiding something. The officer approaches the truck and asks for Barry's ID and registration, the usual thing for a speeding pull-over. Barry obliges, and the officer leaves and returns to his car, Barry still wondering if he should slide the gun under his seat. The officer returns a few minutes later and explains to Barry that he had clocked him at 81 in a 65 but only put down 74 to save him some money. Barry thanks him and tells the officer to have a good night, feeling a little relieved that the officer hadn't seen the .45 on the floor. The officer thanks him and states, "I know how you Jarheads are, but next time you better slide that Colt .45 under your seat, as other officers wouldn't find it cool." Barry thanks him and drives off, noting that he was lucky he didn't go to jail.

Barry attends his parents' 50th wedding anniversary a few weeks later and decides to buy them a Sony video camera to film grandkids and vacations. Barry's father is excited as he is getting older and doesn't always get to some parties and functions. Barry's brother, Wilbur, had borrowed the video camera to take home videos for Dad of his son's birthday party. Wilbur was divorced, and Jacob didn't see them very often because of his health and the long distance. Wilbur had just started his own subcontracting business for framing and stucco, needing a lot of things to get him going. Wilbur had borrowed his father's pickup, a bunch of hand tools from Barry, and of course, the Sony video camera. Wilbur had been working long hours and, one evening, ran out of gas about a mile from the gas station. Wilbur pulled off to the side of the road, got the tools out of the back of the truck bed, and put them inside the cab to prevent someone from stealing them while he was gone to the gas station. He then locked the truck, grabbed his gas can, and started the one-mile walk to the gas station. When he returned to his truck, he noticed police officers surrounding the vehicle, thinking perhaps someone had rear-ended the truck. When he got there, he asked what was going on, and the officers asked him to show his ID. Wilbur obliged. The officers explained that a witness had seen Wilbur putting the tools in the vehicle cab, so they suspected he had stolen them, and they put Wilbur under arrest for grand theft auto, petty theft, and no proof of insurance. The officers never called anyone but had the truck towed and all the tools confiscated for evidence of theft.

Wilbur got bailed out the next day and went to his father to explain the situation. Barry's father, Jacob, called Barry the next day asking if he had receipts for the tools and the video camera, which Barry explained he could come up with in a few days. Jacob took all the titles, receipts, and documentation to the police department the next day. The police department took all the necessary copies but informed Jacob they couldn't release the items until the next day. Jacob didn't understand why, but told them he would return the next day at 3:00 PM. The next day, Jacob went back to the police station, and they returned the tools and video camera, but they told Jacob he would have to go to the impound yard to get his truck. They could have told him that the day before, and that started the point at which Jacob was pissed at the cops. Once leaving the police station and driving to the city impound yard, he finally got to the people in charge of his truck. They explained to Jacob that with towing, impound fees, and storage, he had to pay $748. Jacob got very angry, but because of his age, he couldn't beat someone's head sideways. He tucked his tail, paid the bill, and started his journey home with his truck. The dispatch, perhaps busy or incompetent, forgot to remove the vehicle from the APB stolen vehicle list, and Jacob got spotted by a passing officer. The officer calls out on his radio that he needs backup and starts to pull over Jacob's truck. Jacob pulls over, and the officer steps out of his patrol car, yelling for Jacob to exit the truck. Jacob states he is not getting out of the vehicle, and they can kiss his ass. Backup arrives about that time, and 4 officers are out of their patrol cars, pointing weapons and screaming for Jacob to put his hands on the roof and exit the vehicle. Again, Jacob tells them to kiss his ass. They repeat the command numerous times. Nobody really knows how long it would have gone until shooting would have started, but about that time, dispatch comes on the radio to inform the officers that the vehicle in pursuit has been removed from the stolen vehicle list. The officers then inform Jacob that they are sorry and that he is free to travel home.

After arriving home, Jacob realizes that the video camera has a bunch of police video and an officer's child's birthday party on the hard drive. That was the reason for the delay in the return of confiscated items, and Jacob thinks about starting a lawsuit but never does, as it isn't in his nature.

I fought the Law

Barry decides to set up a family camping trip so everyone can get together and relax, as the times have been busy and a little hectic. Both Barry and his brother Wilbur have been busy with their businesses, so Barry asks his dad if he could reserve a camping spot, as they are only available on Wednesdays each week, unless there is a no-show during the week. It's a popular camping area, one that Barry and Wilbur have many childhood memories of, but because of the times, it's quite crowded during the summer months. To eradicate bugs and disease, they make each camper move out of the campground every Tuesday while they spray the sites, and then they can move back in on Wednesday mornings. That's a great time to find a spot, as most campers schedule their stay until Tuesday and then move on to new grounds. Barry's plan is to come up after work on Wednesday evening, and his brother will follow about 10 PM, as his drive is farther. Jacob goes up early Wednesday morning at about 7 AM and finds a nice spot that will hold both campers, then pulls in to fill out paperwork. Jacob puts a 6-pack of Squirt, a lawn chair, and a newspaper on the picnic table, fills out the envelope with his name, and stuffs a 90-dollar check for the 3-day stay. Jacob stays for a couple of hours reading the newspaper, drinking a Squirt, and enjoying the view before heading home for the day, bringing the pay stub home to Barry. Barry gets packed up, and his son starts the 1-hour drive to the lake at approximately 5:30 PM.

Upon arriving at the lake, Barry looks for the camping spot that his father has paid for, only to find that it is taken by a huge 36-foot motorhome. Barry knocks on the door of the motorhome and asks the people if they perhaps have the wrong spot. The couple states that they talked to the camp host and that the host had told them they could have the spot, as it was obviously not being used. Barry went to the camp host and asked the same question, wondering why they would allow someone to take the spot after it was already paid for. The host said he didn't make the decision; the camp manager did, and that she was in the main office next to the Regional Forest Service office. Barry drove up and parked in the parking lot, getting more upset as he was dragging a camper and his son around the lake. Barry went inside and asked for the manager and was directed to her office. The camp host had already radioed the manager to explain who Barry was. Barry introduced himself and stated that his father was the one who wrote the check for the camping spot. The manager explained that there was nothing she could do—the spot was taken, and the situation was closed. Barry was furious, but he realized it now involved more than just him and his camper; it involved a whole list of people. He told the lady that he was angry and had a whole family coming for a yearly camping trip, but he realized that meant nothing to her. Barry told her she was lucky she was a woman, as he had no problem going to jail for assault, but if she wanted to return his money and items, he would leave the lake. The manager said that she had her guys throw all the items in the trash and that he would have to write a letter asking the company in Arizona for a refund. Barry said that would be the ONE thing that would keep him from leaving the resort, as he was not leaving until he was paid in full. She called the Forest Service next door by radio and instructed them that she needed help with a rowdy camper. Barry knew he didn't want to be in close quarters, so he went outside to wait for the Forest Service backup.

As Barry stood in the parking lot, vehicles pulled in, and four Forest Service personnel got out, including one female. The personnel weren't ready for what they thought they were doing, and even as the lake manager was yelling at them from the second floor of her building, they weren't ready to get beaten unconscious for her. The young Forest Service girl told the manager that they were not trained for this and to call the local sheriff, as she knew the police were more suited to controlling the situation. The young female employee could tell Barry was extremely angry and that he had been in worse situations before. Barry tried to get the service personnel to engage, but they kept their distance until the sheriff arrived. The local sheriff pulled into the parking lot and asked Barry what the problem was. Barry explained that he got ripped off by the lake manager. Upon hearing this, the manager screamed that she wanted Barry arrested and thrown in jail. Barry called her every name in the book and told the sheriff that all he wanted was his money back, but now it had gone too far, and he wasn't leaving until a bunch of people paid him back with skin. The sheriff told Barry that he was too old for fighting and would just have to shoot him if things came to that, at which point Barry's son started to cry. Barry's son was only 7 years old and wasn't worried about his dad fighting, but wasn't prepared for gunplay. As Barry's son cried, Barry told the sheriff that he was lucky he was with his son because without him, he would have taken his chances. Barry smiled at the young Forest Service kids and drove off in his pickup, yelling profanities at the manager.

Barry drove past the sheriff and said, "If you see my crazy brother, tell him I will be at Stanley Lake campground." The sheriff nodded that he understood. Barry drove 30 minutes to the next lake and found a spot to pull into with his camper. A couple of hours later, Wilbur showed up with his camper and kids, stating that a Forest Service employee had asked if he was Barry's brother and that he was camping here at Stanley Lake. Wilbur said the kid had said Barry was the craziest SOB he had ever seen, but that Barry had stated his brother was the "crazy" one. Wilbur and Barry laughed, with Wilbur saying they hadn't been drinking… yet!

The next morning, Barry was sitting outside drinking a cup of coffee by himself when the sheriff pulled into the campsite. Barry figured he was coming by to either give him a ticket or arrest him for the previous day, so he wasn't friendly when the car pulled up. The sheriff approached the campsite and said he was glad Barry had backed out of fighting the night before. He apologized for the manager's actions and stated it wasn't right, but everything had gone to shit since Idaho sold the lake to Arizona. He opened his passenger truck door and pulled out a 6-pack of Squirt and a new Boise Statesman newspaper, stating that he knew this didn't make it right, but it proved what side he was on. Barry shook the sheriff's hand and thanked him for what he had done, joking that the whole world had gone to shit except for the two of them.

Barry and Wilbur went to the lake to swim later that morning, meeting Jacob, and the rest of the family showed up later that afternoon. Despite the rocky start to the trip, everyone had a great time camping, telling stories, and swimming for the week. Barry tried to get Jacob to stop payment on the check, but Jacob refused to do it, thinking they might retaliate in some way, costing more than 90 dollars when it was over. Barry knew Jacob would have gotten more involved, but at his age, he found it easier to bow out.

It's never a dull moment, it seems, with Barry's younger brother Wilbur. Wilbur takes after his grandfather when it comes to drinking, something Barry walked away from years ago. Wilbur has his run-ins with the law, and because Barry and Wilbur are very close, it affects Barry every now and again. Barry and Wilbur are always hunting and fishing, so they tend to loan guns and gear back and forth depending on the day. Wilbur gets pulled over for drinking and driving with some of Barry's guns in his vehicle, and the cops confiscate them. Barry gets two guns confiscated on one occasion that were with Wilbur, and when Barry finds out a few weeks later, he learns he no longer owns the guns. The police department has a policy stating that the true owner of the guns only has 14 days to collect confiscated guns, and Barry is 4 days too late. Barry asks what happens to the guns, whether there is some sort of auction, but the police are not willing to answer any questions. Barry knows the precinct and their practices, so he writes it off as another loss for him and his brother. The police have made another score, a common habit when it comes to guns.

Times seem to be getting busier everywhere, and it's no different at Barry's shop. The population is growing, but parking lots aren't expanding, which creates a problem for all businesses. Barry's shop is located beside a gas station and convenience store. At first, it's nice to have something that close, but as traffic increases, it makes things a lot worse. Barry has applied for a permit to put a fence up along his property, but it continues to get denied because of the grandfathered gas station and the danger it could create due to a new design for old customers. Barry is always complaining to the store owner, but the store owner does less each time a problem arises, as he hates Barry, mostly due to the fight about the fence a year earlier. Barry has had customers' cars run into, people stealing things, and customers stealing cars without paying.

Barry talks to the police each time something happens, mostly because he needs to fill out a police report for insurance purposes. The police don't like the situation; it's not their problem, but Barry complicates it by telling them to patrol the area more often and put more pressure on the gas station for cameras and paying attention. The police tell Barry that the place has been like this for 50-75 years, so that's just the way it's going to be. Barry always brings up laws that have changed in America over the last 50 years that were upheld as law for 200 years. One of the police officers had shot and killed a homeless man who had attacked him with a frying pan a few years ago, and Barry never lets the officer slide for his actions. Barry works out at a gym where a few of the officers also work out, so they knew Barry was three times their strength. The only officer who liked Barry was a young woman who was very strong herself. Barry occasionally spotted her at the gym. She knew he was a nice guy unless you crossed him, and truth be told, she had a crush on Barry. She rode a Harley Davidson chopper to the gym each day, and Barry would comment on how she handled the bike and how strong she was. The police don't seem to give Barry any support when it comes to his shop and the activities that take place there—a far cry from "protect and serve."

Barry decides to purchase a new paint booth because the old one was too short for 4-wheel drives. While installing the new booth, which took a couple of weeks, the fire marshal was constantly stopping by to tell Barry he better not paint in the building until the booth was fully functioning. Barry can't run his business without painting, so he has his painter spray vehicles after work hours. The fire marshal knows what's probably going on with illegal activities, so he calls OSHA to monitor Barry's business. One morning, an older gentleman pulls up to the shop just before opening hours and asks to see the shop's production. The man introduces himself to Barry, and Barry gets a bad attitude towards him, as he knows OSHA is going to fine him thousands of dollars without the paint booth in working condition. The man knows Barry is pissed off and goes to his vehicle for about half an hour to let Barry cool down. It's not this guy's first rodeo with people who hate OSHA.

The man comes back to the door of the shop and asks Barry if it's okay for him to continue his observation. Barry answers that it is. The man goes into the shop for an hour or so, taking readings and checking equipment. Barry had his air compressors in a separate shed outside, and the OSHA rep liked that and told Barry so. He explained that if he had been painting in the shop, he would have gotten fined 20-30 thousand dollars, but he could tell the shop wasn't fully functional. The man then told Barry that there was a faulty electrical outlet in the shop, so he would have to pay him 450 dollars. Barry wrote him a check, and the gentleman thanked him for letting him check the facility out. The man handed him a business card and told him that he tries to help small businesses as long as they're trying to conform. Barry felt lucky the day cost him only 450 dollars, and he informed the officer that he could have the booth done by Monday for him to reinspect.

Barry doesn't rely on the police most of the time; he's always felt that he and his family could take care of their own. He has a 1968 Mustang in his parking lot that gets run into during the night, and no one knows how it happened. This infuriates Barry, as the car must be fixed for free, and Barry hates losing money that other time would reimburse. Barry takes some of his equipment, trailers, skid steers, and a backhoe, and positions them exactly on the property line between the two properties. It makes an impervious wall, and customers can't get into the fuel pumps if they're towing a trailer. Barry's neighbor is furious. He calls the police, and they ask Barry if he will move the bucket of his backhoe, as it's in the right-of-way by 4 feet. Barry agrees and moves his backhoe bucket back into the parking lot by 4 feet. The owner is still pissed but can't do much about it without a lawsuit, other than tell his customers that Barry is just an asshole. Certain people who buy beer and goods next door let Barry know he's being a "dick" about the parking as they walk to the store.

Barry doesn't care much; he's concerned with protecting his customers and his business checking account.

Things continue as usual until a few weeks go by and one of Barry's customers, an 80-year-old woman, can't get her car past a semi-truck parked in Barry's parking lot. Barry had been in the back and hadn't noticed the delivery truck had parked in his lot. The semi-truck likes to park in Barry's lot because it is easier to park, and he doesn't block the store's gas pumps with his trailer. Barry asks one of his employees if they would help the elderly woman get out of the parking lot, as Barry went to talk to the truck driver next door. The delivery truck would not only block the gas pumps to deliver goods, but the driver would also have to back down the alley to park if he didn't park in Barry's lot. Barry understands why the driver wants to park there, and if the owner next door or the truck driver had come and asked for permission weeks in advance, Barry probably would have let them, if they promised to get it done quickly. Neither the owner nor the truck driver asked; they just decided they would do what they wanted, as the owner had been there for many years and claimed seniority. Barry doesn't understand who would feel that way, as property is property in his mind.

Barry goes into the store to ask the delivery driver to move his truck back to the store property and off his property. The truck driver tells Barry he will move it when he's finished and not until then. Now Barry is pissed, and he tells the driver that if it isn't moved in 30 seconds, Barry will move it himself. The truck driver tells Barry not to touch his rig, or there will be hell to pay. Barry laughs and says, "You don't know me very well." Barry goes out of the store, walking towards his backhoe, gets in the cab, and starts the engine. The truck driver now understands Barry is serious, as Barry drives towards the semi.

The driver yells at Barry, "Stop the backhoe!"

The truck driver warns Barry that he is calling the cops if he doesn't stop, then realizes Barry doesn't care about stopping as he informs 911 on the phone. Barry hears the truck driver screaming into the cell phone that Barry is destroying his truck. Barry moves the rear of the semi out into the highway, and about that time, a young girl, a possible meter reader, pulls up in a police Ford Ranger, jumps out, and yells at Barry to stop. Barry stops the backhoe, and the young lady approaches the backhoe door, telling Barry he must stop or he's going to get arrested. Barry tells the girl to call the next town for backup, as this town doesn't have enough cops to get him in cuffs. For some reason, the girl runs back and does exactly what Barry instructs her to do. Barry's backhoe is not strong enough to lift the engine of the semi tractor, so he can only slide it into the highway and off his property. He returns his backhoe to where it was parked, shuts it off, and starts walking towards his company office. At that time, police cars start pulling into his parking lot, one sliding sideways from the high rate of speed. One officer jumps out of his patrol car, pulls his pistol, and screams for Barry to freeze and give him his name. Barry just keeps walking and points at his company truck, yelling that his name is on the side logo of his truck, and continues into the office door. Once inside, 8-9 police cars pull into his lot, running around and talking to the truck driver, but not one came into the office. The police all did their due diligence and then left the area except for the two officers who were the first to respond. At that point, they came into the office and asked for his ID, which Barry handed over, asking if they needed his insurance. The officer then explained to Barry that they would be back to arrest him once they figured out what charges would be applied. Barry told them he would be waiting for them to return, but he felt as though they would end up kissing his ass when it was all over. The officer slapped his black leather gloves into his other hand

and stormed out of the office. One of Barry's friends, Brad, had gone into a convenience store at the time it was on the police radio, and Brad asked the clerk what all the chatter was. She stated that some crazy guy at Hailey Auto Body was getting arrested. Brad laughed and told her, "He's not crazy, just don't piss him off."

Barry never heard from the police again, although each week the police would escort the delivery truck to unload groceries to protect the delivery truck driver. The police would make sure the truck driver parked in the city right of way and didn't encroach on Barry's property. Barry always wondered why they never protected his lot thefts the way they protected the semi that was illegally parked in his lot weeks earlier.

People are funny. Barry always wondered why humans never pay attention to the outside world, but they don't. A few weeks after the big semi episode, a man backed his truck right in front of Barry's front business door. Barry thought it was a customer just getting ready to drop off a vehicle. After about 30 minutes, with most of the shop filled with exhaust fumes, Barry went out to ask the man what he was doing. The man exclaimed in broken English that he was waiting for his boss. Barry told him to drive over to the other side of the parking lot, but Barry wasn't sure if the man understood.

After another 30 minutes, Barry was pissed and went out to make sure the guy understood to get off his lot. Barry went outside and slapped the driver's window so that the guy would know he was serious, not realizing how hard he swung. He hit the window hard enough to break it. The Hispanic man's boss pulled in a few minutes later and freaked out that Barry had broken his employee's side window. The small Asian man came inside the office and started screaming at Barry for being racist and something about Arnold Schwarzenegger, and that if Barry ever did that again, he would chop off his balls. Barry picked him up and threw him out of the shop onto the asphalt, causing him to hurt his arm.

The man called the police. The police told him to contact a lawyer, as they had no authority on private property. Barry knew the police were done with anything that went on in the body shop parking lot.

Barry has a good friend named Frank who owns a small clothing shop and sells authentic Mexican candies and chips. He has set up the ability to wire funds outside the United States using MoneyGram. He also cashes paychecks for local employees for a fee. He tells Barry that the check-cashing business makes him more money than all the other parts of his business. Frank tells Barry that he is charging the same as the banks, but he gets a lot of Hispanic people because he doesn't require them to have a checking or savings account. Frank doesn't know it, but some of the banks call the FBI to check into the business for fraudulent activities. They raid Frank's houses and business a few months later and arrest Frank for tax evasion and weapon charges. Barry knows it's BS, and that it was made up because someone was making more money than the local banks. Another great American system. Barry goes to court to testify as a friend at the FBI court in Boise. Because Frank owned two houses and had his mother, father, and three brothers living in one of them, the whole family was arrested. Since Frank's parents were over 60 years old, the police arrested them but let them bail out the same day. Barry testified about his friendship and told the judge that the three brothers could live at his house under house arrest rather than leave 15-year-old kids in jail. The judge agreed with Barry's offer and instructed a police officer to set them up with ankle bracelets and transport them to Barry's address. Barry went home, and the police followed with the boys a couple of hours later. After about 3 months, the parents and the boys were found not guilty, but Frank was sentenced to 5 years for failure to obtain a banking license after a plea deal.

Fear is one of animals' biggest emotions. It affects all beings and keeps us alive when justified. Humans struggle to know when it's justified, even when common sense tells us its threat is low. One day, while running a piece of equipment at work, Barry finds that none of his employees are showing up for work, even though it is past starting time. He tries to call some of them with no luck, so he leaves a voicemail. After an hour or so, just when Barry is starting to freak out, one of his employees comes walking in from the back of the property. He is upset and informs Barry that the other employees were arrested that morning. Barry remembers seeing 20-30 police cars from different counties parked at the restaurant that morning at an early hour, and begins to wonder. The day goes on, and Barry just continues with business as usual with just one employee. Later that evening, Barry sees on the news that the state had done an immigration sweep, arresting most of the Hispanic people in the county. Barry studies to find out that it was an attempt to find illegal aliens and question them for domestic threats. Barry understands but finds it irresponsible for the government to blanket people based on nationality. Barry learns that his employees are in Mexico City and will be flying back home after they prove U.S. citizenship. After 3 weeks, his employees returned to work, telling Barry that they had lost their company coats and cell phones. Barry questioned them about how the whole thing could have allowed them to get sent to Mexico City. They told Barry the police just arrested them as they came out of the house and then threw their coats and phones in the trash at the police station. They destroyed their green cards and loaded them on a bus for Mexico. Once they arrived in Mexico City, they had to wait to retrieve new green cards to return to the U.S. They booked a flight and came home to the United States. The whole thing cost the employees 3 weeks of work, a plane ticket, and cost Barry 3 new coats and 3 new cell phones. Barry didn't know if that was a win/win or a lose/lose.

Sometimes, no matter how right you are, you can't catch a break. Barry is driving along a local highway and sees what he thinks is a woman's purse. Barry turns around, pulls off the road, and sure enough, it is a purse with everything most women would have in it—cash, her paycheck, her ID and Visa cards, and luckily, there is a phone number on her personal checks. Barry calls that number and leaves a message as he continues to drive home. Barry goes home and takes a shower, as he is leaving to go out of town for 5 days to Portland. About that time, the phone rings, and it is the husband of the young lady whose purse Barry found. He is quite upset that Barry had found it in the street and seems as though he doesn't believe the story of just "finding" it. Barry tells him whatever and asks what he wants to do with the purse. He informs Barry that he will be at Barry's house in 1 hour to retrieve it. Barry tells the guy he is leaving in 2 minutes and cannot wait around as he must be on time. The guy is furious that Barry won't wait, so Barry tells him he will just take it to the police station a block from his house. The guy tells him not to do that, but Barry hangs it on the door handle because nobody is at the police station after hours. One good deed for the day turns into Barry getting his ass chewed by an unthankful loser.

Crime Pays

Business owners always deal with thieves and liars, but most people are good for their word. It's hard to run a business or personal life with a negative attitude, but every day, dishonest people are born. A promise, a handshake, or even a contract doesn't curb people who are hell-bent on thievery. Even wealthy people don't comply at times—like when a woman's vehicle sustains significant damage to the front end of her Yukon, and she had dropped it off for repair. When the vehicle was finished, Barry called her to let her know it was ready for pickup. She showed up in an Uber, came inside the office to pay for her Yukon, and then realized she had left her purse in the condominium. She stated she was only thinking that her keys were in her Yukon, so she didn't need anything else, and said she would be right back to pay with her Visa. Barry was in the back of the shop working, and his secretary just didn't think the lady would lie to her, especially in front of her two young children. She did lie and never returned to pay her bill, stiffing the shop for the repairs. Barry did get ahold of her ex-husband in NYC, and he confirmed she had never paid for anything. She lives off his child support. Barry knows he won't be seeing the $8,000 fix anytime soon. Living in a very rich area, Barry learns one thing: thieves come in every size and shape.

Barry's house is big, with a large backyard that incorporates a 10-person hot tub. During the summer months, Barry turns the tub heater off so the kids can use it as a swimming pool rather than a hot tub. The kids love it, and some days, they invite other neighborhood kids to come over and swim. If they spill a little water that day, Barry just fills it up for the next day. One day, Barry's family notices that a young girl is watching through the fence as Barry's children swim. The girl is holding a baby, still in diapers, that is only around one year old. Barry's kids ask if it's alright for the neighbor kids to come over and swim. Barry agrees. Barry's family invites them to swim, but the older sister states she will need to ask her mother when she gets off work. The next day, the neighbor children come over and explain they can swim once their mom meets Barry. Barry goes next door, introduces himself, and explains that the kids are welcome to join his kids to swim during the hot summer days. The neighbor thanks Barry and tells him that she can't afford a babysitter but feels safe with Barry being a neighbor to her children. Barry tells her she is welcome and lets her know that if she needs anything, she can let his kids know. The kids play for a couple of months, and Barry's wife feeds all the kids most days, including the neighbor girls. One weekend, a friend of Barry's stops by to visit, asking where the other kids came from. Barry explains they are the neighbor kids and explains that their mother works during the day, so the kids hang out at his house. Barry's friend's wife is kind of a Karen (a nosy bitch) and feels it's her duty to call Child Support Services on Monday to report abuse. It's a decision Barry doesn't agree with but feels most people with problems of their own tend to inflict justice on others.

CSS goes by on Monday to the young neighbor's house and arrests the family, causing the young mother to lose her kids. The young mother comes by a few days later to scream at Barry and his wife, with Barry trying to convince her that it wasn't them. A couple of days later, Barry's custom 51 Merc is keyed on both sides—this was the young neighbor's idea of getting back at Barry. Barry tells his friend that he and his wife are never allowed on his property again and prepares to repaint his custom car.

Poor Economy

Big business always trumps small business, and Barry knows that this statement has always been true. Some people think the banks value their customers, but it's only the money that they care about.

Barry was working on a complete paint job at the shop, which required stripping a Mercedes car to bare metal. It was a one-hundred-thousand-dollar classic car, and the owner wanted it perfect. The car was in the shop for a few months, and as it was nearly finished, Barry pulled it outside to bake in the sun for an afternoon. A man in a new F150 pulled up and asked Barry if that was a '62 Mercedes hardtop. Barry confirmed that it was, and the man exclaimed how rare they were. Barry agreed, and then the man said it was beautiful before driving off.

The next few days, the car was assembled with all the glass and chrome, but the owner wasn't responding to Barry's calls. Barry spoke to his wife, and they discussed the possibility of renting a storage unit to hold the car for a couple of weeks until the owner picked it up, just to prevent any scratches or damage. They didn't return from lunch, and soon the police and a tow truck arrived to pick up the car. Barry asked what was going on, and a banker approached him, informing him that the car was being repossessed because the owner hadn't made a payment in four months. Barry told the police and the banker that nobody was taking that car until he got paid for the paint job. The police explained to Barry that the bank had seniority, and he wouldn't get paid until the car was auctioned off. If there was any money left over, his shop would receive a check. Barry replied to the police and the banker, saying, "The American saying 'we the people' is just a line of bullshit, I guess." Everyone looked at Barry, seeing him as both right and insane in one glance. Barry was sure the bank got paid, especially with the beautiful custom paint job, but he never did.

Even when things are bad, it doesn't mean there aren't good moments, and sometimes money does return a favor. One morning, a gentleman backed into another man's car. Barry didn't see it, but the two men pulled up to the shop and discussed the accident. The gentleman said he had backed into a Mercedes and would like an estimate. Barry got the information and presented the estimate to both parties. The car was an expensive one, and although it had only chipped the paint and cracked the taillight, the repair cost $800. The men agreed on the repair, and the gentleman stated that he was from out of town and would just like to pay the invoice and be done with it. Barry agreed, charged his Visa card, and told the other person involved that he would call him when the taillight arrived, offering to fix the chip while he waited. They all agreed, and Barry mixed the touch-up paint and worked his magic on the small chip. Once the repair was done, neither client could tell where the damage had been. All that was left was to wait for the taillight.

Barry explained that most parts are delivered overnight, but with import imported cars, one can never be sure. He told the customer to plan for a week or so. The client said it was just a small crack, so he could get by for a week or so. They parted ways, and Barry ordered the taillight from the Mercedes dealership in Salt Lake City. The next day, the dealer called to inform him that the taillight was on national back order and would take at least a month to arrive. Barry checked with a few recyclers, but since the car was only six months old, availability was zero. Barry broke the bad news to the man, and he was very unhappy. Barry told him it wasn't anyone's fault, but it was what it was. A month later, the man was extremely upset, stating that if the taillight wasn't there in two days, he wanted his money back. Barry told him that probably wouldn't happen, as he wasn't about to absorb the cost of a Mercedes taillight, and it wasn't even his money involved. Another week passed, and the man and his wife showed up at Barry's house one evening, demanding their money. Barry told the man he was way out of line bringing business to his house, and to leave before Barry "stomped a new mud hole in his ass." The man responded that he was a retired Army boxer and loved beating up big guys. Barry told him to get out of his car and come onto his property, but Barry's wife had already called the cops as she knew things were going to get ugly. Within a few minutes, the cops arrived—Barry's house was only four blocks from the police station—and dispersed the scene. A few days later, the taillight finally arrived. Barry took it to the police department, along with the touch-up paint and $22 in cash for installation labor. Barry told the police captain that if the man came to his shop or house, he would kill him before he got out of the car. To make sure everyone in the station understood his anger, Barry screamed that he would gut the man's wife with a 10" Bowie knife. Barry never saw the man again, and it was bittersweet for him.

Barry has always supported the community and financially supported both the state police and the DARE program each year. He hated drugs and didn't want kids to struggle with them for the rest of their lives. He even funded the math department by purchasing rulers and protractors for students in the local high school.

Barry had done a complete paint job on a Chevy Suburban, changing the color from an old, faded green to a bright lemon yellow.

Once the vehicle was finished, Barry called the owner to say the Suburban was ready for pickup. The man showed up just as unmarked police cars pulled up. The man was arrested for drug trafficking, and the vehicle was confiscated. Barry, once again, didn't get paid, and this time it was even an insurance claim. The check needed to be signed by the customer, but the insurance wouldn't accept an unsigned check. The vehicle went to the DARE program for auction, and Barry stopped by multiple times to try to get his money from the DARE organization. That never happened, but Barry made it clear that he would never support DARE or the police again.

Barry has never liked big business, especially banks. It's probably a sentiment shared by most Americans since the Great Depression. It seems banks live by their own rules, while consumers live by another set. Even after Americans bailed them out, they tend to laugh in the faces of the common people.

Barry had a client who had his boat painted and wrote a check, but that check came back from the bank as NSF (non-sufficient funds). Barry called the gentleman, who explained that he had forgotten to pull funds from another account and would just write and mail him another check. He mailed another check, then stopped payment on it to avoid being charged for writing a bad check. Barry sued him and won a judgment a few months later when the defendant didn't show up for the court date. Barry struggled to find the guy and retrieve his money for the bad check. One day, a year or so later, one of Barry's employees saw the man at a parts store, writing a check for a purchase. After the man left, Barry's employee asked the store manager to see the check and took a picture of it. The employee returned to the shop after lunch and showed Barry the picture. Barry freaked out and asked how he got the photo. The employee said, "The less you know, the better." Barry took the picture and ran to the bank with the judgment from the lawsuit. The bank issued him a cashier's check, and Barry skipped out of the bank in excitement. He ran to his bank and deposited the funds, thinking that this was the one time he finally came out on top. About 30 days later, his bank called him at the shop and informed him that what he did was illegal, and they would have to reverse the funds. Barry wondered how the world worked if that was considered an illegal act. Nevertheless, Barry knew he'd never see the money.

Sometimes people get pushed into illegal acts by mistakes of the law or the lack thereof. Barry had a young lady whose muffler had fallen off her car, and it was as loud as a dragster when she pulled into the shop. Barry told her they didn't normally do exhaust work, but could put on a cheap muffler for her to get by. She said she didn't have the money until Friday, so Barry told her that it would only be $60, and she could pay him on Friday. Barry's employees put on the least expensive muffler the parts store had and sent her on her way, her car now quiet as a mouse.

She never stopped in to pay for the muffler but instead told everyone that knew Barry that his shop hadn't even put on a tailpipe, and her kids were sick because of it. Barry got tired of her BS and decided to pay her a visit one afternoon. He removed the muffler from her car. He imagined her shock when she got off work and heard her vehicle start up with that loud noise again. The next day, the police stopped by and arrested Barry for petty theft, instructing him not to contact the client.

Barry went to court a few weeks later and told the judge that not only had she not paid for the muffler, but he had been just trying to help her out by getting the work done correctly at a muffler shop. The judge told him that once the muffler was placed on her vehicle, it became her property, paid for or not, and that he would have known that if he were an attorney. Barry stood up and started walking out of the courtroom, stating that if he had gone to college for another semester, he would have his job. This pissed off the judge, who fined Barry the maximum amount—$300.

Barry had purchased two trucks at a police department auction in Oregon and brought them back to his shop for repair. He did the required repairs and placed the trucks at the front of his property for sale. Barry had gotten these vehicles cheaply and hoped to make a good profit by selling them. The next morning, a female meter maid stopped by the shop and told Barry that he couldn't sell the vehicles, as the city had a law prohibiting the sale of vehicles while they were parked on city property. Barry argued that the property was his and not the city's, so he could sell the vehicles if he wanted to. She argued with Barry for quite a while, then threw a fit about it being a public parking lot and drove off, telling Barry she would return with papers to shut him down.

Barry just laughed as he went inside, thinking that the girl was crazy and wondering what she would make up when she returned. A couple of hours later, a very polite woman called and told Barry that he was fine to sell on his lot. She didn't even act like she had been yelling and confrontational just hours earlier. Barry wrote it off as bi-polar behavior.

Barry hired a painter with a good reputation for high-quality work. The guy was skilled in many areas but was second to none when it came to painting and pinstripes. He worked for Barry for about two months and then asked Barry if he could borrow $5,000 to move closer to the shop, as his family had been living with his mother-in-law. He said he had a custom car worth over $20,000 that he could put up as collateral. Barry said he would need to see the car but would think about it, noting that it would be nice for him not to have to drive an hour to work.

The next day, the guy drove the Pontiac Firebird to Barry for him to see, and Barry agreed to loan him the money, provided he would pay it off in five months. Barry had him sign a loan contract and hand over the car title, then wrote him a check for $5,000. After the next paycheck, Barry deducted $1,000 from his pay, as agreed, but Barry could tell his employee wasn't happy about the deduction. That weekend, the employee took his custom car out of the shop and cleared out his tools, leaving a note saying he quit.

Barry went to his employee's new house and asked what was going on, explaining that he wanted the car back until the money was paid. Barry told him that he could still pay him in the remaining four months, but he wanted the car back in the shop. The ex-employee's wife had already called the cops, and they showed up around that time. The wife showed the cops a new title, claiming they had lost the original title years ago and had to get a replacement. The police told Barry that his title was now null and void, and that he must leave or face arrest.

Barry complied, but he was really pissed off, realizing the whole thing had been a scam from the start. The couple had applied for the lost title before they even secured the loan, and Barry had been played just so the guy could rent a new house with a body shop on the property. Barry vented his anger by calling the woman everything from overweight to being LDS, as the cops stood by and listened. Most people didn't want to get involved when Barry was pissed, even with his threatening nature.

Barry went about his business for the next few months until one evening he ran into the ex-employee at a local bar. Barry didn't start anything, but there were sure to be faces made back and forth for the time they were inside. Barry didn't drink, but the ex-employee was extremely intoxicated, and his wife had a big mouth when she was drunk. Barry decided to leave, but as he walked outside to the steps, he felt someone punch him in the back, which was kind of funny since Barry's back was the largest muscle on his body. Barry turned around, threw the ex-employee to the ground, and punched him in the face four or five times until one of Barry's friends, Harold, asked him to stop the fight. Barry stopped and left the area in his truck. Harold told him that he could see death in Barry's eyes, as he was so pissed off.

The police questioned witnesses and determined that Barry had only used self-defense. About two months later, Barry was served with a lawsuit from the ex-employee, claiming he had been viciously assaulted. Barry wasn't happy about getting served, as the lawsuit demanded $1 million, describing the man as permanently harmed. After months of litigation with both lawyers, Barry finally went to court as a defendant for assault. It only took one day. The other lawyer struggled with lies from his client, with Barry being the only witness in the room who hadn't been intoxicated that evening. The lawyer tried to argue that an object must have been used since no human could inflict that kind of damage with a bare fist. Barry suggested they go outside and reenact the fight, but the judge scolded him for making ridiculous outbursts.

Barry's friend Crazy Harold testified that it was just Barry's fist, and that the ex-employee was lucky Harold had been there to stop the fight. Barry won the suit and was very happy with the decision, as it could have gotten ugly.

Barry has a lot of friends in the business and occasionally recommends them for different work. One of Barry's friends, Kurby, does mechanic work in his garage and is struggling with a carburetor that he can't tune on a truck. He asks Barry if he could adjust it if he brings it over. Barry tells him he will do it the next day.

Kurby drops off the truck, and Barry gets it running, explaining that he had to completely rebuild the carburetor to make it work. Kurby thanks him and says he will do him a favor someday when he picks up the truck. Kurby asks Barry for the carb kit part number, and Barry hands him a business work order that includes the number.

A few weeks go by, and the police stop by to serve Barry with a lawsuit from someone he had never heard of before. After a few phone calls, Barry realizes that it is the gentleman that Kurby had him rebuild the carburetor for. Barry's not sure why he's involved, but as the investigation shows, Kurby had used Barry's invoice as fraud to bill out the client. Barry could have had Kurby arrested for fraud, but they are friends. The man didn't really have any idea that Kurby was not Peterson's repair shop. Barry is furious and tells Kurby that when they go to court, he will tell the judge that Kurby stole the invoice.

Kurby acts as though he will go along on the day of court, but he realizes his name isn't even mentioned in the lawsuit. Kurby goes MIA on the day of court, and Barry is left holding the bag at court. Barry learns that the engine Kurby had rebuilt for the gentleman blew up about 50 miles after he picked it up. The man had explained that all the oil ran out of the engine in the first 10 miles, but he kept driving to Boise as he needed to get there.

At a stroke of luck for Barry, the judge tells the guy it was his duty to check the oil and stop the truck if he knew it was leaking oil. The judge dismissed the case and told the guy to work it out with Kurby. Barry never knew what happened after that but let Kurby know he was on his shit list and not to come for favors again.

Sometimes people think Barry has a hatred for cops, but he has a hatred for incompetent people. If the law is followed and the punishment fits the crime, then he's all about it. One time, while driving down the road, he saw a man running out of the bank, heading toward an alley, and then popping out at a motel and going inside a room. Barry thought things looked a little strange, so he turned around as cops were pulling into the bank. Barry recognized one of the officers and yelled out to him if he was looking for a robber. The cop replied, "Yes," as he knew Barry also. Barry states that the officer should check room 6 at the motel down the street. They arrested the guy a few moments later, and Barry was mentioned in the paper a few days later—not by name, but with a community thanks.

Barry had the same secretary for years at his shop, but she decided to go back to school, so she had to quit. Barry was sad to see her go, as she was just the best at her job, but she told him she would train a new girl, saying she thought she knew someone to replace her. The new girl came to work the next week, and the two of them held down the fort as the training took place. The new girl was smart and caught on quickly. She was an attractive, friendly girl, so customers seemed to like her.

After a few months, Barry and his wife decided to go on vacation, so they booked a cruise out of California. Barry and his wife had a great time on the vacation, but on the way home, one of Barry's employees called him on his cell, stating that he couldn't cash his paycheck. Barry told him he wasn't sure why, but would be home in another day, so he would have to wait until then.

Barry got home on Sunday and went to the bank first thing on Monday morning to see what was going on. The bank was being very unhelpful, telling Barry that he was overdrawn and needed to deposit more money to get his employee's checks cashed. Barry states that he should have over $20,000 in his account and needs help finding out where it went. The banker gets in Barry's face and tells him that everyone who is overdrawn has that same attitude. Barry explodes and tells the banker that he is going to kick his ass and work his way down to the tellers. The banker pushes a silent alarm, and wouldn't you know it, the cops show up minutes later.

The cops tell Barry to leave and never come back to the bank, and if he calls, he is not to use any threats. Barry agrees and heads back to the shop. He is pissed off, so his wife calls the bank and talks to one of the tellers who has known Barry for 20 years. The teller gives the information about what had happened in the last 20 days and blurts out that someone was ripping off the account. Barry's wife does even more investigating for the next few days, and even though the bank wants to close Barry's account, she begs them to wait a few more days.

Barry finds out that the new secretary, Erica, had stolen $35,000 in both Visa charges and forged checks. Barry fires Erica and tells her she will go to jail for theft, then calls the cops to send an officer over to the shop. An officer stops by the shop but explains to Barry and his wife that they don't handle fraud cases in the county, and that he would call the police from another area that deals with fraud and embezzlement. A few days later, the fraud department police show up to give Barry and his wife advice on what to do. They explain that arresting a 20-year-old girl would ruin her life and that it would be better to try to recoup the money without filing charges.

A day or two later, Barry gets the copies of the checks that were cashed when he got his mail and reviewed them for fraud. All the checks were signed completely wrong, with misspellings, and the most notable issue was that they were right-handed. Barry takes the forged checks back to the bank and tells the bank manager that these checks need to be refunded to his account, as he signed a signature card when he opened the account, and these signatures aren't even close.

Barry tells him that he takes business losses seriously and knows it hurts, but he needs his money refunded. Barry states that he wants his money by 4:45 PM as it's the right thing to do, and if it doesn't happen, he will be back at 4:59 PM. The banker freaks out, calls the cops, closes Barry's checking account, and signs a restraining order against Barry. The cops serve the restraining order at the body shop, and Barry laughs in their faces, stating, "You think a piece of paper will stop me!"

The bank has five cop cars parked at the bank at 4:30 PM that day, and believe it or not, Barry doesn't get his money. Barry's friends tell him it was the news of the town at happy hour.

Barry's employees like working at the shop and respect Barry in his quest for having a great business. Barry is upset about the way the cops handle taxpayers and criminals in this country. It's as though it's reversed from what the law was originally founded for. After lunch one day, an employee comes back and states that Erica, the ex-secretary, is working for a different bank in town as a bank teller. Barry tells his employee that they probably just saw her vehicle in the parking lot, and she was inside doing some banking. Barry suggests that a bank would do a background check and never hire her in the first place.

The employee says they don't think so, but perhaps Barry is correct. A week later, the same employee tells Barry that he went inside the bank this time and that Erica is positively working as a teller. Barry is infuriated and leaves the shop to go to that bank, arriving a few minutes later. Erica is nowhere in sight, but Barry asks for the bank president. He goes into the president's office and introduces himself, causing the man to jump with joy. The president states that he had wanted to come see Barry but hadn't had time. He tells Barry that Erica had stolen money from the bank, and they had her arrested.

He says that the police had told them the same thing—just let her go—but the CEO told the police department they would file a lawsuit against the city if she wasn't arrested within one hour. Erica was arrested and went to jail, showing Barry the difference between big business and small business taxpayers.

Barry must open a new checking account at another bank to be able to function as a business. He has to use handwritten deposits and checks for the first week or so until the permanent ones come in the mail. One day, Barry's wife deposits a few checks on her way home from work and drops her vehicle off at a dealer to have some service work done.

The next week, the deposit doesn't show in Barry's account, so he calls to see what happened. The bank doesn't show it and tells Barry to bring in the deposit slip, and they will fix it. Barry calls his wife to have her bring the deposit slip by the shop on her way home, and she agrees.

Later that day, she stops by and can't find the slip in her truck after the dealership had changed her oil and cleaned her vehicle the week before. Barry finds himself in the same predicament as before, although this time it was his fault. He talks to the banker, and the banker is short and rude about the mysterious loss of the deposit slip. One of the tellers remembers Barry's wife coming into the bank around that time, as she knows her quite well.

During her lunch hours over the next day or so, the teller reviews the deposits made that month and finds one that resembles the shop's deposit. After a few days, the teller finds the deposit and calls the recipient of that deposit to verify its accuracy. The teller discovers that it was deposited into the wrong account, so she credits the amount into the correct account.

Later that week, the teller is fired by the bank manager for interacting with bank proceedings during banking hours. Barry feels responsible for the girl's firing but chalks it up to another big business policy. Barry calls the bank manager after he finds out and thanks him for taking the time to track down his money. The manager knows Barry is being sarcastic, but he acknowledges him anyway, preventing Barry from ruining another relationship.

The city has a separate sales tax from the state sales tax to generate extra cash to hire more policemen, buy vehicles, and maintain the streets. Barry stops paying this monthly tax, and after a few letters from the city, the tax official calls to see what's going on. Barry tells her that the city has never done anything for him or his business and that they can shove the tax letters up their asses.

She tries to inform Barry that if she doesn't get the money, they will do an audit, and the police will come to collect the money. Barry laughs hysterically and tells her, "Good luck. Let's hope there's gunplay, as I'm tired of the BS."

Law Won

A week or so later, Barry and his painter are standing in the office on a slow day when Barry sees a few police cars pull up on the highway, driving behind a blue four-door sedan. Barry laughs and turns to his painter, stating that this is the American way: using three police cars to pull over a sedan for doing 40 in a posted 35. Barry's painter goes back to work in the shop, and Barry sits at his desk with his legs up on the counter. He watches as his police friend gets out of a cruiser and makes her way to his shop while the other cops wait at their squad cars. Barry wonders what's going on as he watches her walk 200 feet to his office door.

She comes inside, and Barry greets her by saying, "Good afternoon, what's up?" She states that there are some men who need to talk to him, but they want Barry to come to the middle of the parking lot without anything in his hands. Barry knows it's not good, but jokes to her that she's the only one tough enough to come get him. She states that she is the only friend he has when it comes to a badge. They both laugh.

They walk together to the center of the parking lot, and she informs Barry to drop to his knees and put his hands on his head. Barry complies, and the other six officers proceed to where Barry is sitting— some with guns drawn, but two suits sporting .38 Special revolvers, which makes Barry smile. Being a right-brainer, Barry takes in everything in the area, just in case.

The two suits introduce themselves as FBI agents out of Portland, Oregon, and they are there because somebody fears a threat. Barry questions why that would be, as he only does wrong to people who do wrong to him. They tell him the information is confidential, and they can't tell Barry those details, but they will let him know some other details to help him understand why they are there. Barry says, "Okay," and they continue.

The agent tells Barry that they've done an intense background check on him, as the local department doesn't feel they can get the answers they need. The FBI's background check surprises Barry with what they know, and for Barry's brain, it's more of a learning experience than a threat. The agent starts out by telling Barry how many fights he's been in, how many lawsuits he's faced, how many guns are registered in his name, and other financial records. They also tell him they feel he's never recovered from the loss of his son and doesn't care about dying because of it. Barry laughs and says, "While most of that is true, I haven't cared about dying my whole life." He adds that most of the "local department" doesn't like him because he's always right, and the fact that Sara (the female cop) and he outlift them.

Sara laughs, and so do the FBI agents, although nobody else finds it funny. Barry tells the FBI agents that he has worked his ass off most of his life and doesn't really care about going to prison. He says, "It's high time I get my money back from American citizens." The FBI agents tell him he's not going to prison, that he wouldn't like the food, and that he just needs to stop the threats. Barry promises he will never threaten anyone again.

Barry's wife suggests that they close the shop to stop the fighting before Barry gets arrested for life. Barry agrees and moves his tools and equipment to his house. He turns over his invoices to the local credit bureau, hoping to collect some of the $300,000 he's owed. He has a shop at his home, but it's not as big, and some of his equipment must stay outside in the weather. Barry isn't working on customer cars, just his own resto mods, so he only has one car inside his shop.

A few months later, Barry is helping his son by painting a 1968 Chevelle that is his senior project, and the doors are partially open in the shop. A woman drives by at a very slow speed and stares at the work going on. Barry doesn't know her, except than he notices her car parked five or six houses down the street. She drives by every day from work, and Barry waves at her each time he sees her, hoping she is just checking out the old classic cars. She never waves back to Barry, and she couldn't care less about custom cars. She only wants to contact the authorities.

A few days later, a police officer stops by, informing Barry that he can't be running a business out of his home. Barry tells the officer that he isn't running a business but is helping a student with his senior project. The officer leaves but returns a week or so later. Barry figures the lady must have called again, as she had been driving by a lot that week. The officer tells Barry again that he cannot be spraying vehicles with paint in a residential area. Barry tries to reason with the officer, saying that his house and his property are the nicest in town. It's not like he's running a chop shop with old junk lying around. Barry tells him that almost every person in town is spraying their house, their deck, or some other item with paint.

Barry says, "After owning a body shop for decades, I know how many Hispanics in the valley are painting cars for a living." As they're speaking, Barry tells the cop, "I'll make you an offer. If you go and arrest the 50 guys painting in their garage in the city, I'll gladly load up in the bus and go to jail. But if you come back again without those other arrested men first, there will be gunplay." This irritates the officer and causes him to storm out of the shop and drive off. The officer returns a few minutes later and hands Barry copies of the local code and instructs Barry to read them. Barry thanks him, and the officer drives off, leaving Barry a little confused as to why the officer even did that, but he reads them anyway.

A few weeks later, Barry gets a letter from the state tax commission informing him that he is being audited. They tell him he hasn't been paying sales tax, both locally and on internet purchases, and that his cell phones are personal, not business. Barry contacts an accountant, and she explains that businesses are getting charged with internet sales tax even though they were purchased out of state. She also says that cell phone bills are so high for businesses that you can't use them for personal calls. If you do use them for personal calls, they are not deductible as business phones. She persuades Barry to just pay the fine, as he will not win in court to fight it. Before Barry can come up with the money, they have already placed a lien on his house and vehicles.

Barry and his wife sell their home, pay the government, and move to another town where they buy another home. Barry then goes into teaching high school business classes. Strangely enough, before Barry can get his teaching diploma and certificate, he must pay $800 in parking tickets he incurred at the University. He finds his niche; he loves kids, and they love him and respect his wisdom.

www.ingramcontent.com/pod-product-compliance
Lightning Source LLC
Chambersburg PA
CBHW071115120626
46546CB00003B/1347